Be expert with
Map & Compass

The Complete
"Orienteering"® Handbook

New enlarged edition

Orienteering ®

Finding your way—Finding yourself

Science, mathematics—And the divine thing called LOVE:

  Love of NATURE.

Intense exertion—Explorers' pride

Wholesome solitude—And glorious comradeship!

Be expert with
Map & Compass

The Complete
"Orienteering"® Handbook

New enlarged edition by
BJORN KJELLSTROM

Illustrated by
Newt Heisley and Associates

Maps by
U.S. Geological Survey
and Orienteering Services

CHARLES SCRIBNER'S SONS · NEW YORK

Charles Scribner's Sons
Macmillan Publishing Company
866 Third Avenue, New York, N.Y. 10022
Collier Macmillan Canada, Inc.

Library of Congress Cataloging-in-Publication Data
Kjellström, Björm, 1910–
Be expert with map and compass.
Includes index.
1. Orientation.   2. Maps.   3. Compass.   I. Title.
GV200.4.K53 1976   796.4'2   76-12550
ISBN 0-684-14270-8 Paper
ISBN 0-684-16413-2 Cloth

Macmillan books are available at special discounts for bulk purchases
for sales promotions, premiums, fund-raising, or educational use.
For details, contact:

Special Sales Director
Macmillan Publishing Company
866 Third Avenue
New York, NY 10022

12 11 10 9 8 7 6 5 4 3

Printed in the United States of America

CONTENTS

FOREWORD

Since the first edition of this book was published in 1955 it has sold well over a quarter of a million copies in the English language alone. French and Italian editions have also been a success. So, apparently it did fill a need. But we cannot avoid the fact that in the more than twenty years which have elapsed since the first publication things have happened in the field of Orienteering which make an updating and expansion of the book necessary.

The basic teaching of map-and-compass use is very much the same, but the part of the book which covers the Orienteering program with its practicing games and competitive sports events has been modernized and substantially expanded. That section now gives complete basic information on all aspects of Orienteering without going into all details. Those who would like to learn more, for example in the fields of Orienteering instruction, organization of competitions, or map drawing, or who wish to have a complete reference library, will find a great deal of special literature available through the Orienteering Services in the United States and Canada or through the respective Orienteering Federations.

The two purposes for which this book was originally written remain the same:

First, to give YOU a chance to join in the fun which is being experienced by an ever-increasing number of outdoorsmen and women through an imaginative use of map and compass in finding your own way and being your own guide, whether along highways or through the wilderness.

And second, to attempt to make you so enthusiastic about the potentialities of map-and-compass work in Orienteering that you will want to help *others*—whether members of your own family, friends, or outdoor-interested people of all ages—share your enjoyment.

To achieve these purposes, every effort has been made to present the fundamentals of map and compass as plainly as possible—not just for your own education, but also for simplifying the job of teaching these fundamentals to others. To help you master the skills yourself and to enable you to help others master them, a large number of specific practices have been included, suitable for self-testing and for group games and projects.

Skill with map and compass cannot be learned from book reading only. It must be learned through practice—through the actual handling and using of the tools of Orienteering, map and compass, in combination with a steadily developing power of observation. To get your practice under way as quickly as possible, this book is provided with a training map, a training compass, and a practicing protractor. The use of these items from the very beginning in conjunction with your reading should move you quickly into the world of mastering map and compass in your newfound experience with ORIENTEERING.

Although the main function of this book is to provide for the learning of the fundamental skills for traveling outdoors by map and compass, it is also intended to promote among young and old an enthusiasm for Orienteering as a sport. Those readers who might become interested in competitive Orienteering racing (cross-country running with map and compass) will find all the information and hints they need in the last part of this book—not only for active participation in the sport but also for the organization and execution of successful Orienteering events.

This handbook of Orienteering is the result of many years of personal experience in this fascinating field, including active participation and instruction in competitive Orienteering racing on an international level.

My interest in Orienteering goes back to 1928 when, in my native Sweden, my brothers—already successful orienteers—inspired me to join the sport. In my first race—in the beginners' class—I finished next to last. In my next big event a few months later, I brought my team to a leading position in an Orienteering championship race. It may have been this incident that made me an orienteer for life and eventually made me one of the missionaries for the promotion of Orienteering on trips to different parts of the world, resulting in the introduction of Orienteering to the United States in 1946 and to Canada in 1948. During the first couple of decades after Orienteering was introduced in North America, interest in it grew at a very moderate

rate. It is only within recent years that it has taken a major spurt and is now one of the fastest growing sports of our continent.

In this development, and in the writing of this book, I owe a large measure of thanks to a great number of organizations and individuals. They have contributed in various ways, directly or indirectly, by providing ideas and by fostering an enthusiasm for the sport of Orienteering. Among organizations the following should be specifically mentioned: American Association for Health, Physical Education and Recreation; National Recreation Association; American Camping Association; Boy Scouts International Bureau; Boy Scouts of America; Canadian Boy Scouts Association; Girl Scouts of the U.S.A.; Canadian Girl Guides Association; The International Orienteering Federation; The United States Orienteering Federation; and The Canadian Orienteering Federation. Also such agencies as the National Cartographic Information Center of the Geological Survey, U.S. Department of the Interior; Department of Education, Ontario, Canada; Department of National Health and Welfare, Physical Fitness Division, Ottawa, Canada; the U.S. Army Infantry School; the U.S. Air Force Academy; and the Physical Fitness Academy of the U.S. Marine Corps.

Many individuals have also shared in the writing of this volume. There are simply too many to mention here. I do owe special thanks, however, to William Hillcourt, "Green Bar Bill" of the Boy Scouts of America and *Boys' Life* magazine and well-known writer on outdoor life, who contributed a great deal by editing the text.

To him and to all supporters and helpers, my sincere thanks!

And now—may you, the reader, by studying this book and by following its suggestions, lay a foundation for an interest in outdoor life and in Orienteering which will remain with you always. Have fun!

BJORN KJELLSTROM
Pound Ridge, New York

INTRODUCING:

The Art of Orienteering

With every passing year, America is becoming more and more out-door-conscious. Her roads are teeming with cars, her parks with visi-tors, her outdoor trails with hikers and campers.

Most travelers go by route numbers or trail signs, but an increasing number of them strike out by themselves along little-known paths, or cross-country.

Whichever way you travel—whether you follow the main lanes of our country or its byways—you will get far more fun out of your experience if you are thoroughly familiar with the use of map and compass.

"But why bother with map and compass," you may ask, "when the roads are numbered, the trails clearly marked?"

Because map reading today is an essential part of any person's basic knowledge—whether for traveling or for keeping track of events in our own country and around the world.

Because the ability to use a compass in the field is an outdoor skill that will help make you self-reliant and confident in all your travels.

Because the use of map and compass together opens up chances for greater enjoyment of traveling and of the out-of-doors than you have ever experienced before.

With map and compass as steady companions, the art of Orienteering—the skill of finding your way along highways and country roads, through woods and fields, through mountain territory, and over lakes—becomes an intriguing hobby and an interesting sport, whether you travel alone or with a buddy, with your family, or with a group of like-minded friends.

Map and Compass in Your Everyday Life

Fundamentally, we all make use of maps and compass directions in our everyday lives—consciously or unconsciously.

When you sit down to plan a trip, whether by automobile, rail, ship, air, or on foot, you get out maps or charts and try to figure out the shortest way, the best way, or the way that will take you past the greatest number of interesting places. Then, on the trip, you consult your maps repeatedly to check where you are and where you are going.

When someone asks directions or when someone gives them to you, your brain automatically attempts to draw an imaginary map of the location. In your mind you see roads as lines, rivers as bands, buildings as small squares—exactly the way they are represented on a map.

Map and Compass for the Outdoorsman

The experienced outdoorsman has no fear or uncertainty about traveling through strange territory—map and compass will get him there and safely back again.

Orienteering is becoming more and more popular as a challenging cross-country sport for youth groups: Boy Scouts, Girl Scouts, Explorers.

In family Orienteering, junior may sometimes like a piggy-back ride.

Backpackers use Orienteering to find their way through wilderness areas.

Foresters, surveyors, engineers, prospectors, men in the armed services all require thorough training in Orienteering with map and compass. The yachtsman needs a sound knowledge of chart or map and compass to navigate our waterways.

If you are a hunter or a fisherman, you will have done much traveling to your favorite hunting spot or trout stream by map and compass—unless you have depended on a guide. In territory you know well from having traversed it again and again, the lay of the land and the different directions will be part of your working memory. When it comes to new territory, on the other hand, you have probably pored over maps and compass and have used them to find your way to the best hunting ground, the best-stocked lake.

If you are a backpacker, your map and compass will give you a sense of complete independence and freedom of movement. Whenever you feel like breaking away from the trail you are following, you can travel cross-country with utter self-confidence and unrestricted abandonment. You can explore far afield to find the hidden lake you may have heard about, the mountain glade, the waterfall, knowing that your map and compass will get you safely and surely back on the trail.

If you are an athlete interested in cross-country running, Orienteering will add new spice and new dimension to your pursuit. In addition to the physical gymnastics of regular running, Orienteering calls for mental gymnastics in using map and compass for choosing your route instead of following a route laid for you, in figuring out ways and means of overcoming obstacles, in deciding what shortcuts to take to get to your destination in the shortest time possible.

And if you happen to be a leader of Boy Scouts or Explorers, of Girl Scouts or Camp Fire Girls, or a camp counselor taking your campers on a cross-country hike, or a teacher with your pupils on a field trip, you will readily recognize the need to know the proper use of map and compass so that you may transmit that knowledge to the boys or girls in your charge and help them get along safely and securely in the outdoors. In addition, you will know that map study and compass use can be a source of a great number of interesting games and projects and competitions for meeting room, club room, or class room, and for hiking trail and camp site.

If you are none of these, but simply a vacationer in a state or a national park, or a Sunday stroller in the woods, you will still discover that a map and a compass will increase the fun of your vacationing or your hiking.

Map and Compass for the Family

Orienteering is the perfect sport for the whole family. It is a sport for all ages that can be enjoyed at leisure. Young children take to Orienteering like ducks take to water: reading a map is easier and more fun than reading the alphabet. Teenagers find a special physical-mental challenge in Orienteering. Parents through with work and household chores find relaxation in Orienteering. Even the older generation can join in the wholesome fun of "getting away from it all" for a while.

A vast majority of American families enjoy weekend "outings" and spend summer vacations together. An ordinary hike in the country becomes an adventure when plain walking is combined with the cerebral exercise of finding the way by map and compass, exploring off the beaten track. And a vacation trip becomes even more exciting when, afterward, you tell about your experiences penetrating areas where no one else has walked, discovering natural beauties that no one else has seen.

Family Orienteering is not just taking "a hike with a purpose"—it is also learning about nature. Family Orienteering is one of the finest ways of teaching young and old to appreciate the environment in which they live, getting them to know and to love nature and, thereby, giving them the desire and determination to protect nature and all our natural resources.

The Romance of Orienteering

Aside from enjoyment there is a real satisfaction in mastering the art of using map and compass.

There has always been a romantic fascination to persons who could find their way through the wilderness and over hidden trails—the Indian, the pioneer scout, the guide, the tracker, the explorer. There seems to be a mysterious power behind the remarkable capacity for pathfinding.

In the old days, pathfinding was well worth admiration. It was based on a highly developed power of observation and of remembering—reading the signs of mountain ridges and rivers and vegetation, wind directions and cloud movements, the position of sun and moon and stars.

Today, pathfinding is much simpler with a good map and a dependable modern compass.

Where the old-timer learned his skill the hard way over a great number of years, the outdoorsmen of today can learn the secrets of Orienteering in a matter of hours.

And when you have mastered the skill, it sticks.

It will help you on all your outdoor expeditions. It will make you feel safe and certain in the wildest territory. It will make it possible for you to cut down travel distance and travel time through shortcuts. It will challenge you to explore out-of-the-way places of special interest. It will show you the way to new camp sites and fishing lakes and hunting grounds.

And, eventually, it may turn you into a protagonist for Orienteering as a sport—helping others to enjoy themselves in exciting, competitive cross-country racing.

Go!

Kipling wrote of the challenge of a special yearning that lies deep within each of us:

Something hidden. Go and find it. Go
            and look behind the Ranges—
Something lost behind the Ranges.
            Lost and waiting for you, Go!"

For an orienteer nothing needs to be "hidden" or "lost behind the ranges." You can find what is there by using the skills of Orienteering.

So: "Go!"

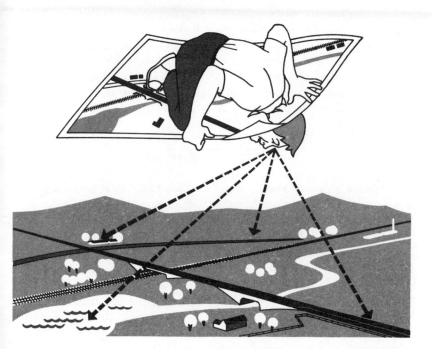

PART I

Fun with Maps Alone

There is a tale in the Arabian Nights' Entertainment of a magnificent contraption: a magic carpet. The lucky owner could seat himself on his carpet, recite the proper magic formula—and suddenly the carpet would rise in the air and carry him wherever he wanted to go.

Imagine yourself traveling cross-country on that kind of a carpet—or on its modern equivalent, an airplane. It is a bright day—visibility unlimited. The sky above is blue. Below, the ground spreads before you in a multicolored crazy quilt pattern. First everything is just a jumble of details. But soon certain things begin to stand out.

That straight ribbon down there, for example, must be the

highway—Route 66, or whatever it happens to be. Now it crosses a wide, winding band—obviously a river. You can even make out the bridge as two short lines—the bridge railings. The rectangles are house tops, the dark-green masses surely forests. Things look different from what you are accustomed to—yet you recognize them in their reduced dimensions.

WHAT A MAP IS

If you took a camera shot of what you see below and later printed it up in a fair size, you would have a photographic "map" of the area over which you flew—with a lot of confusing details and with distortions toward the edges because of perspective, but a "map" nevertheless: *a reduced representation of a portion of the surface of the earth.*

The modern map maker uses aerial photographs and checks them through surveys in the field. But in the final map, he simplifies details into representative signs he calls "map symbols" and flattens out the perspective so that every section of the map looks the way it would appear looking straight down on it, and so that all distances are in the same proportion on the map as they are in the landscape.

What Kind of Map to Get

Of all kinds of maps, probably the maps you know best are automobile maps you pick up at your local service station. The majority of these are designed to cover a whole state; others may cover several small states or the main cities of a state.

In designing state maps, the state is reduced to fit a convenient paper size, folding into the familiar rectangles that fill so many automobile glove compartments. This means that many different scales are used. A map of New Jersey, for example, may be scaled so that 1 inch on the map equals 5.2 miles of highway. On a New York map, 1 inch may equal 11.2 miles of roads. A Michigan map may have a scale of 1 inch equaling 14 miles, while on a map of California 1 inch may equal 21 miles.

These maps will help you find your way from town to town, from city to city, but they won't tell you whether you have to travel uphill or downhill to get there. Automobile maps are all planimetric—from the Latin *planum*, flat ground, and *metria*, measurement—and have no indications of elevations. It is obvious that they will contain too few details to be of much assistance in Orienteering.

Topographic Maps

The kind of map that will serve you best is called a "topographic" map—from the Greek *topos*, place, and *graphein*, to write or draw: a drawing or a picture of a place or an area.

Such topographic maps are available for large areas of the United States and of Canada. In the United States they are prepared by the U.S. Geological Survey of the Department of the Interior and are often referred to as USGS maps; in Canada, by the Surveys and Mapping Branch of the Department of Mines and Technical Surveys.

What Scale to Pick

Each topographic map is drawn to a specific scale. A scale is the proportion between a distance on the map and the actual distance in the field—or, stated another way, the amount that a distance in the field has been reduced for inclusion on the map.

For the sake of simplicity, these map scales have been developed in such a way that it is easy to measure map distances with an ordinary ruler: inches and fractions of inches. One unit measured on the map means so many units in the field, one inch so many inches.

The three scales most commonly used are the scales of 1 unit to 250,000 units, 1 unit to 62,500 units, and 1 unit to 24,000 units.

On the map, these proportionate scales are indicated by a fraction:

$$1{:}250{,}000 \text{ or } \frac{1}{250{,}000}, 1{:}62{,}500 \text{ or } \frac{1}{62{,}500}, \text{ and } 1{:}24{,}000 \frac{1}{24{,}000}$$

The larger the fraction (the fraction 1 divided by 24,000 is obviously larger than 1 divided by 250,000) the larger and clearer the details shown on it. But on the other hand, the larger the fraction the smaller the territory covered by the same size map sheet.

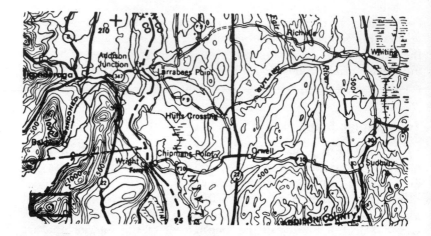

1:250,000 maps will assist you in finding new places to explore. Compare the small
rectangle at lower left with the maps on pages 11 and 12.

But why these specific fractions? The reason is simple and suggests
the map scale best suited to your needs:

1:250,000 Maps—The scale of 1 inch to 250,000 inches is almost exactly the scale of 1 inch to 4 miles. The correct figure would be
253,440—a number that would require a lot of unnecessary work in
surveying. These maps cover an area of 6,346 to 8,668 square miles.

A map on the scale of 1:250,000 will give you a general idea of the
geographic features of your region. It will assist you in discovering
points of interest within a distance of 100 miles and will prove valuable in planning trips and expeditions.

1:62,500 Maps—The scale of 1 inch to 62,500 inches may seem cum-
bersome until it is realized that 1 inch on the map to 62,500 inches in
the field means almost exactly 1 inch on the map to 1 mile in the field.
To be completely correct the scale should really be 1:63,360, since
there are 63,360 inches to the mile—but 62,500 is close enough for
most purposes and certainly simpler in surveying. Also, this scale is
an easy multiple of the 1:250,000 scale.

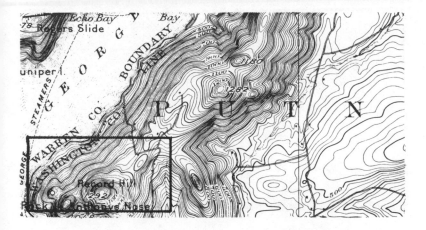

1:62,500 maps are helpful in giving you a general idea of the lay of the land in your area. Compare the rectangle at lower left with the map on page 12.

Maps on a scale of 1:62,500 are available of areas of average public interest. Each map covers an area that ranges from 195 square miles in the northern part of our country to 271 square miles in the southern states. These maps are being replaced by the 1:24,000 scale series.

A map of your locality on the scale of 1:62,500 would be particularly helpful if you intend to cover your area intensively or to locate suitable terrains for a variety of Orienteering events.

1:24,000 Maps—If you choose the inch for your measuring unit, 1 inch to 24,000 inches means that a distance of 1 inch on your map is 24,000 inches in the field. That number of inches translated into feet becomes 2,000 feet—a measurement easily used in surveying.

Maps on a scale of 1:24,000 are made of areas of general public interest. They cover an area ranging from 49 square miles (along the Canadian border) to 68 square miles (in southern Texas and Florida).

For finding your way in a limited area within a radius of, say, 4 miles, and for general Orienteering, the map of a scale of 1:24,000 would be your choice. For a sample, see page 12.

For maps specifically designed for Orienteering, see page 190.

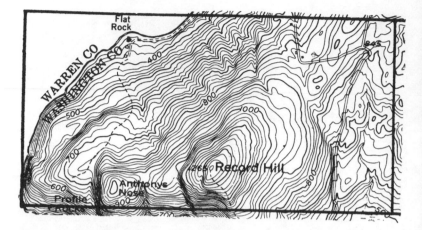

1:24,000 maps are best suited for Orienteering because of the great number of details they contain. Compare this map with the maps on pages 10 and 11.

Where to Get Topographic Maps

United States Maps—You get your topographic maps through the U.S. Geological Survey—in these two steps:

1. Your first step for getting a map of an area in the United States is to drop a postcard to:

> National Cartographic Information Center
> 507 National Center
> Reston, Virginia 22092

(you will find such a postcard, ready for mailing, in the envelope in the back of this book) and request a *Topographic Map Index Circular* of the state in which your area is located, and the Geological Survey booklet on *Topographic Maps*. This material is free.

The Index Circular contains a map of the whole state divided into rectangles—"quadrangles." Each quadrangle map covers a certain area and is designated by the name of a town or some natural feature within the area.

2. Study the Index Circular and decide which maps you need. Then send in your order, specifying "woodland" copies, and remit by money order or check. The prices will be found in the index.

For maps of areas located EAST of the Mississippi River send your order to:

> Branch of Distribution
> United States Geological Survey
> 1200 South Eads Street
> Arlington, Virginia 22202

For maps of areas located WEST of the Mississippi River send your order to:

> Branch of Distribution
> United States Geological Survey
> P.O. Box 25286 Federal Center
> Denver, Colorado 80225

Canadian Maps—For maps of areas in Canada, write to:

> Canada Map Office
> Energy, Mines and Resources
> 615 Booth Street
> Ottawa, Ontario KIA OE9

Other Maps—For areas not covered by regular topographic maps, your best source of information is:

> National Cartographic Information Center
> United States Geological Survey
> 507 National Center
> Reston, Virginia 22092

This center can provide information and ordering instructions for maps produced by many different agencies, including the United States Forest Service, National Parks Service, and others.

WHAT THE MAP TELLS

The map is the outdoorsman's "reader." If you know how, you can read a map as easily as you can read a book. It will tell you what you want to know about the geographical features of the area in which you intend to travel. It does this under five categories—the five Ds of map reading:

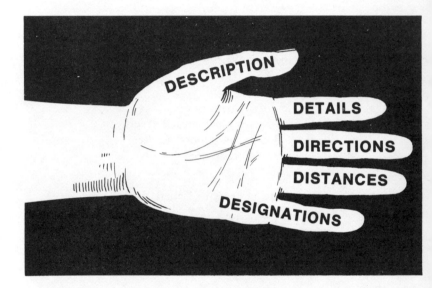

To know what is meant by these five headings, unroll the topographic map you ordered, spread it out flat, and take a good look at it.

Your map didn't arrive yet? Well, don't let that delay your map study. In that case, open up the training map in the back of the book and use that. This map is about one-third of the map surface of an actual U.S. Geological Survey topographic quadrangle map on the scale of 1:24,000—part of map number N4345-W7322.5/7.5, to be exact. In printing this map section for this book the margin was trimmed, but the descriptive matter of the margin was retained; it is inserted in the text that follows in such a way that you will know exactly to which item the text refers.

Description

The description of the map is found in its margin. So let's take a trip the whole way around the margin of a representative topographic map and read all the information pertinent to the use of that map.

Name of Map Area

The type in the top margin contains the name of the main feature on the map—a town, a lake, a mountain, or some other prominent

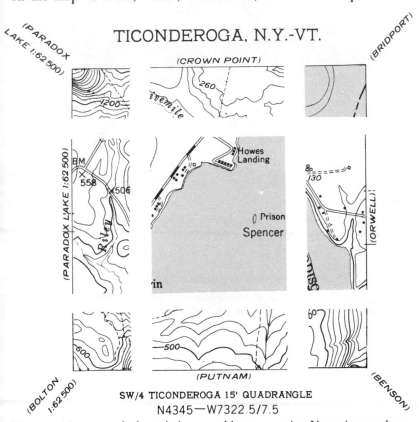

TICONDEROGA, N.Y.-VT.

(PARADOX LAKE 1:62 500)

(CROWN POINT)

(BRIDPORT)

(PARADOX LAKE 1:62 500)

(ORWELL)

(BOLTON 1:62 500)

(PUTNAM)

(BENSON)

SW/4 TICONDEROGA 15' QUADRANGLE
N4345—W7322.5/7.5

The name of your map is shown in its top and bottom margins. Names in parentheses give you designations of neighboring maps.

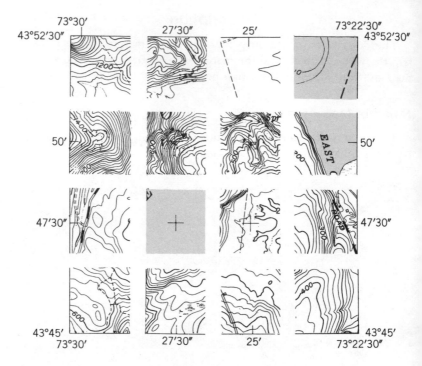

Numbers at top and bottom are longitude degrees; numbers at sides, latitude degrees.
Note cross-marks where connecting lines intersect.

location. That is the quadrangle name used in ordering the map.

This name is repeated at the bottom, with the number of the map.

In small type at top and bottom, at each side, and at each corner are the names of the quadrangles that border on your map. Those are the names you'll use if you want to order maps of the neighboring areas.

Location

Your map is a reduced section of some spot on our globe. But where on that great sphere? Your map tells you.

At the top and bottom lines that frame the map area, and at each side, are small numerals and tiny lines that jut into the map from them. With the help of these numbers and lines you can find the exact place on the globe where your area is located.

If you connect the tiny lines at the top of the map with the corresponding lines at the bottom, you are drawing *meridian lines* that run true north to true south—lines which, elongated far enough, would hit the North Pole in one direction, the South Pole in the other. The numbers attached to these lines are degrees of longitude, figured westward from the zero degree line that runs through Greenwich, England.

If you connect the tiny lines at one side of the map with the corresponding lines at the other, you are drawing *parallel lines*—lines that run parallel to the Equator. The numbers at these lines are degrees of latitude, figured northward from Equator in the Northern Hemisphere, and southward from Equator in the Southern Hemisphere. The Equator itself has the dubious honor of having the zero degree.

Longitude and latitude—care to remember the difference? Then think of their origin: both of them are from Latin words used by the

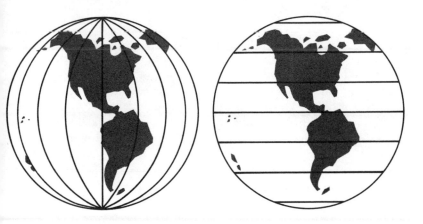

Meridians indicating longitude run from pole to pole; parallels indicating latitude run around the globe. Zero longitude is at Greenwich, England; zero latitude is Equator.

"Longitude" and "latitude" are from Latin words used to indicate the size of the Mediterranean Sea. Longitude lines give the length of the Mediterranean.

Romans to indicate the shape of the Mediterranean Sea—the lines that cut the length of it: *longitude;* and the lines that cut the width of it: *latitude.*

Dates

At the bottom of the map are some dates of importance to you as a map user: to the left, for instance, is the information: "Aerial photographs taken 1942. Field check 1949-1950," and to the right simply "1950" (see illustration on page 55).

The map before you was developed from aerial photographs taken in 1942, drawn and checked by surveyors in the field during the period between 1949 and 1950. The edition you have was printed in 1950.

Well, a number of things may have happened in the area covered by this map since the field check in 1950. If a town is shown, it has probably grown. The road through town may have become a highway; the swamp north of the town may have been dried out; a dam may have been built across the river to form a lake.

So keep in mind that your map was correct for the year it was checked, and don't worry too much if a few changes have been made since then. Just take the possibility into consideration when you plan your traveling through the area.

Details—Map Symbols

To show the details of a landscape, different signs are used—*map symbols*. Map symbols are mapping's alphabet—they spell out the lay of the land. These map symbols are not arbitrary marks. On the contrary, the people who invented them made every effort to have the signatures look like the things they represent.

The main symbols used on topographic maps are pictured on the pages that follow. All of them are found in the Geological Survey's free folder, *Topographic Maps*, mentioned on page 12.

For Orienteering purposes you are mainly interested in four types of map symbols, each with its own distinctive color:

> *Man-made features*, or *cultural features*—BLACK
> *Water features*, or *hydrographic features*—BLUE
> *Vegetation features*—GREEN
> *Elevation features*, or *hypsographic features*—BROWN

Man-Made Features

Under the category of features made by man we have roads and trails, houses and public buildings, railroads and power lines, dams and bridges, and boundaries set between areas. These features are shown on the map in BLACK—with the exception of heavy-duty and medium-duty highways which are sometimes overprinted with RED to distinguish them from less important roads.

Generally speaking, the symbols for man-made features are shown much larger than they should be. This is done for clarity. A road 20 feet wide, for instance, on a 1:24,000 scale map, should be only one one-hundredth of an inch thick—obviously much too thin to be very distinct. Instead, it is shown as a double line. If measuring on a map involves a road, use the middle of the road as the actual point of measurement. Improved roads are shown by solid double lines; unim-

Hard surface highway, heavy duty . . . .

Hard surface highway, medium duty . . . . . red

Improved dirt road . . . .

Unimproved dirt road . . . .

Trail . . . .

Bridge, road . . . .

Footbridge . . . .

Ford, road . . . .

Ford

Fd

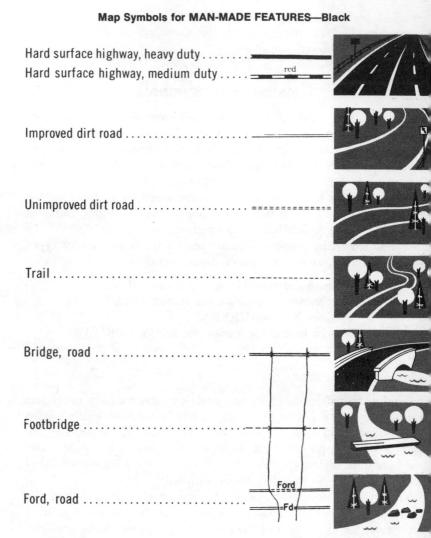

proved roads (in Orienteering referred to as "tracks") by dashed double lines; trails (or paths) by dashed single lines.

Railroads are indicated by full lines with tiny cross-lines to suggest railroad ties.

Map Symbols for MAN-MADE FEATURES—Black

Single track railroad . . . .

Multiple main line track railroad . . . .

Buildings (barn, warehouse, etc.) . . . . ▫ ▫ ▭ ▨ ▨

Buildings (dwelling, place of employment) ▪ ▬ ▟ ▨

School . . . .

Church . . . . ⌂

Cemetery . . . . [⸸] [Cem]

Telephone, telegraph, pipe line, etc. . . . . . . _ _ _ _ _ _ _ .

Power transmission line . . . . -·-·-·-·-·-·-·

Open pit or quarry . . . . ⚒

Water Features

On topographic maps, river and canals, lakes and oceans, swamps and marshes, and other bodies of water are printed in BLUE.

Map Symbols for WATER FEATURES—Blue

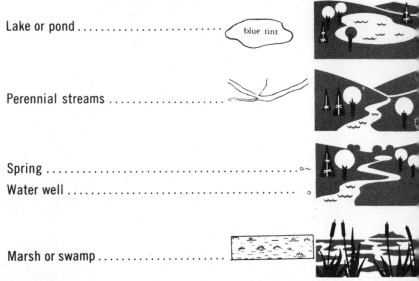

Lake or pond . . . .   *blue tint*

Perennial streams . . . .

Spring . . . .

Water well . . . .

Marsh or swamp . . . .

Brooks and narrow rivers are indicated by a single blue line; larger rivers by a blue band. Large bodies of water are usually shown by a light blue tint with the shore line in darker blue.

Vegetation Features

On recent maps of the United States Geological Survey a GREEN tint is used to indicate wooded areas, orchards, vineyards, and scrub.

For Orienteering purposes it is important for you to know whether an area is wooded or not. Therefore when ordering your map, specify "woodland copy" just to be certain that you receive a map with this green overprint.

Elevation Features—Hills and Valleys

The ups and downs of an area—its mountains and hills, its valleys and plains—are shown on the topographic map by thin BROWN lines called *contour lines*.

Map Symbols for VEGETATION FEATURES—Green

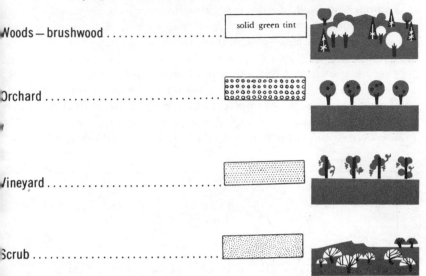

Woods — brushwood	solid green tint	
Orchard		
Vineyard		
Scrub		

While most of the other map symbols are self-evident the contour lines will probably need some explanation.

A contour line, by definition, is an imaginary line on the ground along which every point is at the same height above sea level (although, occasionally, some other reference datum is used).

Unfold the training map in the back of the book. Study those thin brown contour lines. You will discover that every fifth line—known as an *index contour line*—is heavier than the others. These are called *intermediate contour lines*. Follow one of the heavier lines and you will find a number on it. This number indicates that every point along that line is that many feet above the average sea level of the nearest ocean, the Atlantic or the Pacific. Let's say that the number you have found on the contour is 500. If the Atlantic Ocean should suddenly rise 500 feet above its mean level of 0 feet and pour into the landscape, the contour line marked 500 would become the new shore line.

The distance in height between one contour line and the one next to it is called the *contour interval*. What is meant by contour interval? Simply this: that if the water in our imaginary flood should rise by the number of feet indicated on the map as the contour interval, the next contour line would be the new shore line.

The contour interval varies from map to map. On a great number of topographic maps—among them the training map—the contour interval is 20 feet. On a map of a rather level area, the contour interval may be as little as 5 feet; on maps of mountainous territories as much as 50 feet or more—there just wouldn't be room on the map for all those 5- or even 20-foot interval lines. The contour interval of the map you secure from the Geological Survey is found in a note printed in the bottom margin—such as CONTOUR INTERVAL 20 FEET—

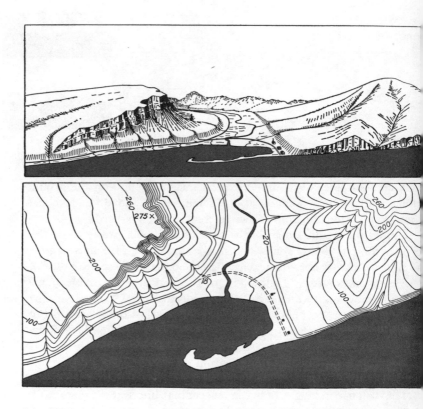

A landscape in perspective above and the same landscape in contour lines below. Note especially that lines are far apart for level land and close together for cliffs.

Map Symbols for ELEVATION FEATURES—Brown

Index contour . . . . ——————

Intermediate contour . . . . ——————

Depression contours . . . .

Cut . . . .

Fill . . . .

Large earth dam or levee . . . .

Sand area, sand dunes . . . .

Triangulation or transit traverse station . . . .   △
   monumented with spirit level elev. . . . .   BM△1062
Monumented bench mark, spirit level elev. . . . . .   BM✕958

but you can figure it out for yourself by studying the numbers on the contour lines of your map.

You'll probably find the contour lines a bit confusing in the beginning, but you will soon look at each hill and mountain in terms of contour lines. Then, when successive contour lines are far apart and evenly spaced they will indicate to you a gentle slope; when they are close together they will tell you the area is steep; when they run together they will show a cliff. When contour lines cross a river or a stream they take on a V-shape, with the point of the V pointing uphill; when they denote a spur or the ridge of a hill they become U-shaped, with the bottom of the U pointing downhill. When the contour lines of a hill are far apart at first, then come close together, the hill before you is a concave hill, easy to climb in the beginning then getting more difficult; where contour lines are close together at first, then get farther apart, you are up against a convex hill, hard to climb in the beginning then getting easier.

The heights of many points—such as road intersections, summits, surfaces of lakes, and benchmarks—are also given on the map in figures which show altitude to the nearest foot.

Simple demonstration of contour lines: dip a rock partway in water, draw water line; dip one inch deeper, draw another line, and so on. View from above.

Map Symbol Practices—Before you continue, test your knowledge of map symbols to make certain that they stick in your memory. And if you are working with others, test them too, turning the testing into interesting games or practices.

On a map, contour lines show gentle slopes when far apart, steep slopes when close together. They become V-shaped for valleys, U-shaped for spurs.

If each contoured area were cut apart, horizontally, from the rest, then stacked one on top of the other, the result would look like this.

The whole area would appear as a natural landscape if the map was turned into a relief, as in this training map by the Army Map Service, Corps of Engineers.

MAP SYMBOL QUIZ   INDOOR PRACTICE

PURPOSE—A quick review of the map symbols to make sure that they are mastered.

TEST YOURSELF—Study the map symbols on page 29. Then, without referring to the illustrations on the preceding pages, write the name of each symbol on the line below it. Don't peek now—but the correct names are found on page 203.

AS GAME—Copy page 29 onto a blackboard, OR cut a mimeograph stencil and run off as many copies as you have players, OR purchase the necessary number of printed Map Symbol Quiz Sheets (from the Orienteering Services—see order blank in the back of the book). Distribute sheets to players, with a pencil to each. Give 5 minutes for filling in the names. Score 5 points for each correct name, up to 85 points for all 17 names correct.

MAP SYMBOL RELAY   INDOOR PRACTICE

PURPOSE—Practice in quick recognition of various map symbols.

AS GAME—Draw the map symbols on page 29 on fifteen 3″ × 5″ file cards. On the back of card number 1, write the name of the symbol on card number 2; that is, on the back of the card showing a road, write HILL. On the back of card number 2 (contour lines), write CEMETERIES; on the back of card number 3 (cemeteries), write RAILROAD; and so on. On the back of the last card (church, school), write ROAD. Make as many sets of cards as you have teams.

   Divide the group into relay teams. In front of each team spread out a set of map-symbol cards, face up. On signal "ROAD—GO!" the first runner of each team runs up, picks up the card showing a road, turns it over, calls off the symbol name on the back of it, "CONTOUR LINES," runs back, and touches off second runner. Second runners runs up, picks up contour lines card, calls out name on back, "CEMETERIES," runs back to touch off next runner, and

MAP SYMBOL QUIZ

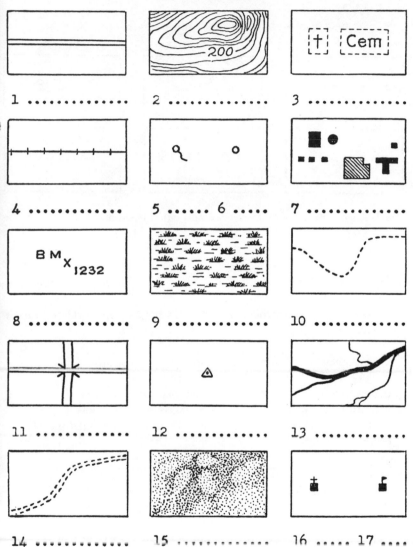

1 ....   2 ....   3 ....

4 ....   5 ...... 6 .....   7 ....

8 ....   9 ....   10 ....

11 ....   12 ....   13 ....

14 ....   15 ....   16 ..... 17 ....

Read instructions for this Map Symbol Quiz on page 28. The objective is to write on the dotted lines the names of the symbols. To use this as a game, have this sheet mimeographed or get copies from Orienteering Services.

so on, until last card is picked up with the runner calling out "ROAD."

The first team to have all cards turned over wins the game.

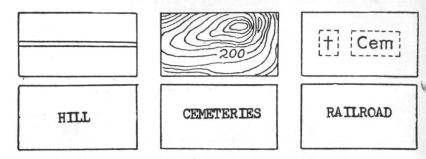

Top line shows the face of the first three cards for the Map Symbol Relay. Bottom line shows the back of the same cards.

IMAGINARY MAP SKETCHING   INDOOR PRACTICE

PURPOSE—To get a general idea of how map symbols relate to each other.

TEST YOURSELF—Study a small section of the training map in the back of the book, then get out a letterhead-size piece of paper and a pencil. Attempt to sketch, from memory, the map section you have just studied, incorporating in it as many map symbols as possible. Particularly important: how roads and rivers run in relation to each other, where buildings are located, where crossroads lead, etc.

AS GAME—Give each player paper and pencil, then dictate slowly the lay of the land of an imaginary territory, such as: "Draw a highway from the top-left corner of the paper to the bottom-right corner. Place a spring at the top-right corner. Start a stream from this spring and run it to the middle of the paper until it hits the road. Make a bridge on the road across the stream. Continue the stream on the other side of the bridge and have it run into a small lake at the bottom-left of your paper. Place a school on the right side of the road, just above the bridge. . . ." And so on, using about a dozen map symbols. When the maps are completed have the players judge each others' maps and vote to decide which is best.

CONTOUR QUIZ   INDOOR PRACTICE

PURPOSE—To be able to read the meaning of contour lines quickly and correctly.

TEST YOURSELF—Read the questions, then study the training map and underline the words below which you believe most nearly describe the actual conditions. Answers on page 203—but don't look now.

1. You are walking the road from Log Chapel to the crossroads north of it. The road is (a) almost level, (b) uphill, (c) downhill.

2. Charter Brook runs (a) from bottom of map to top of map, (b) from top of map to bottom of map.

3. You are walking inland 400 feet on the road from Glenburnie. Your route is (a) a steep climb, rising 100 feet, (b) a slow grade, rising only 40 feet.

4. Sucker Brook is (a) a slow-moving stream, (b) a fast-moving stream.

5. When you stand on the hill marked 400, about one-half mile north of Meadow Knoll Cemetery, you should be able to see (a) Hutton Hill, (b) Meadow Knoll Cemetery, (c) Niger Marsh, (d) Log Chapel, (e) Huckleberry Mountain.

AS GAME—Distribute copies of training maps (from Orienteering Training Kit, see page 210) to the participants. Then begin: "Find Log Chapel, then follow the road northward to the crossroad. Is the road almost level, or are you going uphill or downhill? And how do you know?" First player to put up his hand and answer the question correctly scores 20 points—and so on, until all five questions have been answered for a possible total of 100 points.

CONTOUR MATCHING   INDOOR PRACTICE

PURPOSE—To be able to interpret the outlines of hills and to visualize their contour lines; or, contrariwise, to determine from contour lines how a hill will look in the landscape.

TEST YOURSELF—Study the hill silhouettes and the contour lines on page 33. Match each hill outline with its correct contour configuration by writing down the letter of the hill next to its contour numeral. Check the result against the answer on page 203.

AS GAMES—Three games are possible: (1) *Contour Matching*—Copy all of page 33 onto a mimeograph stencil and run off as many copies as you have players. Have each player match the hills and their contours, as described in the test above. (2) *Outlines to Contours*—Copy only the hill outlines onto a mimeograph stencil and run off copies. The players are then challenged to draw the contour lines of the hills, as seen from above. (3) *Contours to Outlines*—Copy only the contour diagrams onto a mimeograph stencil. Players are to draw the outlines of the respective hills.

Directions

A quick glance at a map will show you the relative direction in which any point lies from any other point. But when you want to find the actual direction between two points as related to the north and the south of the landscape, you need to know first of all what is north and what is south on the map as a whole.

Which Map Direction Is North?

When you place a topographic map before you with the reading matter right side up, you can be pretty certain that what's up is north

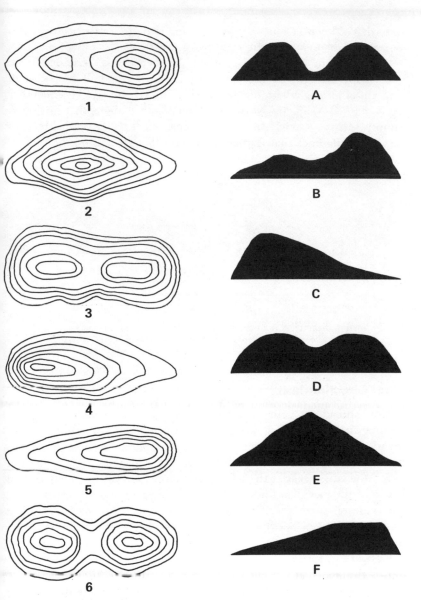

The instructions for the Contour Matching quiz are found on page 32.

and what's down is south. Which means that the left margin as you look at the map is west, the right margin east.

If there is any doubt in your mind about how the directions lie on your map, look in the bottom margin. Here you will find a small diagram of an angle with one leg marked TRUE NORTH—the other leg is marked Magnetic North, but don't bother about that just now. Simply satisfy yourself that the line marked TRUE NORTH runs parallel to the lines that frame the map on the left and on the right.

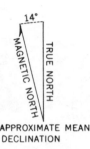

APPROXIMATE MEAN
DECLINATION

The declination diagram in the bottom margin of the map indicates the angle between the true-north and the magnetic-north direction of the map area.

What Direction Is It?

Now spread out your topographic map in front of you—or use the training map in the back of the book. Find a longitude number along the top line of the map frame and the corresponding number along the bottom line of the frame. With a ruler and a pencil, draw a line between the two marks at the longitude numbers. This north-south line is one of the meridian lines described on page 17.

Decide on some specific spot on this meridian line and make that spot your "base of operations" for your practice in determining directions.

First of all, follow the meridian line from that spot up toward the top of the map—any point on the meridian line is directly north of your spot. Follow the meridian line down toward the bottom of the map from your base spot—any point on the meridian line is directly

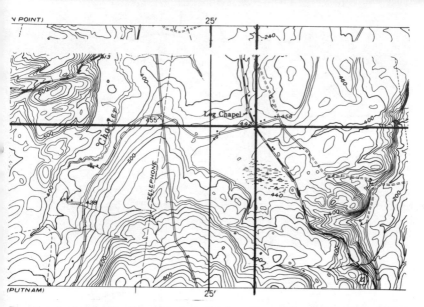

Draw longitude meridian lines, then a parallel through your "base of operations." Find out what lies north and south, east and west, of the base.

south of the spot. Go directly to the left of the spot—any point here is west of the spot. Go directly to the right of it—any point here is east of the spot.

Finding Map Directions with a Paper Circle

But what about all the other directions from your "base of operations"?

To help you determine some of those directions, take a piece of paper, about three inches square. Fold it with sharp folds in half, then in quarters, then in eighths, finally in sixteenths. Round the free edges with scissors. Open up the paper and mark the folds clockwise: North, North-North-East, North-East, East-North-East, East, East-South-East, South-East, South-South-East, South, South-South-

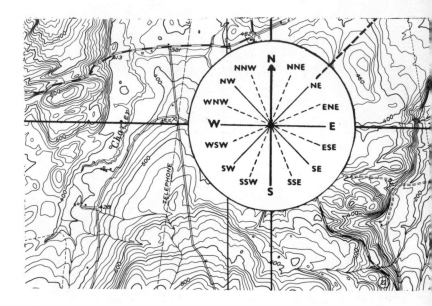

To determine what lies in other directions from your "base of operations," make use of a folded paper circle. Place the center of the circle over your base.

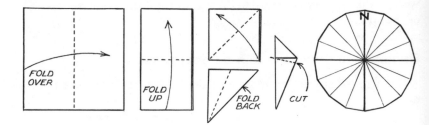

To make a paper-circle protractor, fold a three-inch square of paper in quarters, then into sixteen segments. Trim to circle shape.

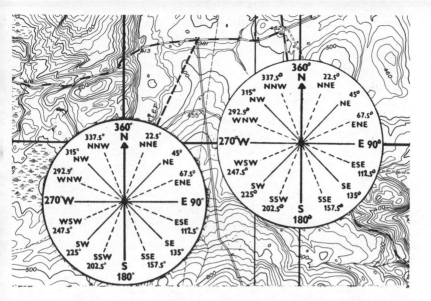

You can turn your folded paper circle into a simple protractor by adding to it the degree numbers of a circle. Zero and 360° coincide.

West, South-West, West-South-West, West, West-North-West, North-West, North-North-West, North—or simply N, NNE, NE, ENE, E, ESE, SE, SSE, S, SSW, SW, WSW, W, WNW, NW, NNW, N. Place this circular piece of paper with its center directly over your "base of operations" with the fold marked North lying north on the meridian line that runs through your spot. Now, to go in different directions from your base you may follow the fold marked NE and continue into the landscape along this north-east "road," or you can go south-south-west, or in any of the other directions (see illustration on page 36).

From Paper Circle to Protractor

The paper circle with its sixteen direction markings is your first step toward using a *protractor*. As you probably know, a protractor is an instrument used for measuring angles. It consists of a circle made from a piece of metal or plastic marked in the 360 degrees of the full circle. The markings start with 0°, go clockwise around, and wind up at the 0° mark with 360°—0° and 360° coincide. Some protractors, for ease in carrying, are semi-circular only.

In using a protractor, the 0-360 degree marking indicates north. South is then how many degrees? 180. Correct! East is 90, west is 270. North-east is 45, south-east 135, and so on. With that information you can turn your paper circle into a primitive protractor: just add the degree numbers at the appropriate direction names:

N—0 and 360	NNE—22½	NE—45	ENE—67½
E—90	ESE—112½	SE—135	SSE—157½
S—180	SSW—202½	SW—225	WSW—247½
W—270	WNW—292½	NW—315	NNW—337½

It is obvious that for exact degree figuring your folded-paper protractor will not be very accurate. Your home-made gadget will assist you in learning the principle of the use of a protractor, but if you want to determine correct readings, you need the real thing. And you will find that in the envelope in the back of the book, in the form of a transparent full-circle practicing protractor.

Finding Map Directions with a Protractor

Bring out the practicing protractor from the envelope in the back of the book and learn to use it for taking degree readings.

Let us say that you want to go exploring in various directions out of your "base of operations." Place the center of your practicing protractor on your base, and line up the protractor's north-south line (its 360°-180° diameter) parallel with the nearest north-south (meridian line) of the map, with the protractor's 360° marking to the north. You are all set now. For any direction you want to go, start at the center, at the point you've picked, proceed toward the degree mark you have decided on, and continue on your way.

But you may not want to go in any arbitrary direction at all. You may have a specific objective in mind—a bridge or a lake. What direction is it? Again, center the protractor on your starting point, lining up the 360°-180° diameter parallel to the nearest meridian line, with

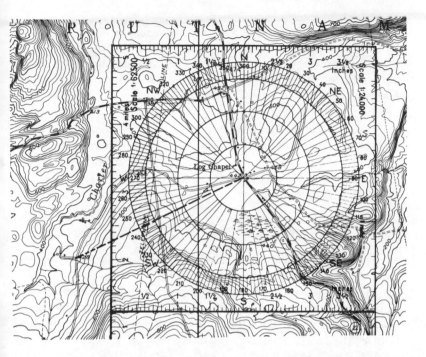

Use the transparent protractor from the envelope in the back of this book for practice in finding directions between various points on the map.

the 360° marking to the north. Now lay a ruler or the edge of a piece of paper from the starting point to your destination. Read the number of degrees where the edge of the ruler or the paper cuts the circle of the protractor. That's the direction in which you want to go, expressed in degrees (see illustration above).

Protractor Practice—Become accustomed to thinking of directions in terms of degrees by using your practicing protractor.

Take Point Bearings   Indoor Practice

purpose—To become acquainted with the use of a protractor for determining directions on a map.

TEST YOURSELF—On page 41 you will find a schematic map showing a number of locations with their relationship to each other and to north as represented by several meridian lines. Using your practicing protractor, determine the degree readings between the following points:

1. From 1 (Church) to 2 (Lake) .... °   6. From 4 to 2 .... °
2. From 2 (Lake) to 3 (Hill) .... °   7. From 1 to 6 .... °
3. From 3 (Hill) to 4 (Quarry) .... °   8. From 5 to 1 .... °
4. From 4 (Quarry) to 5 (Bridge) ...... °   9. From 3 to 6 .... °
5. From 5 (Bridge) to 6 (Cemetery) .... °   10. From 2 to 4 .... °

(Answers are found on page 203.)

AS GAME—Provide each player with a mimeographed or Xeroxed copy of the map on page 41 and a list of the degree readings above, pencil, and a practicing protractor (from Orienteering Kit; see page 210). Give the players 10 minutes in which to determine the degree readings. The player with the most correct answers within the time limit wins.

Finding Map Directions with an Orienteering Compass

In the modern Orienteering compass, the circular compass housing is attached to a rectangular base plate in such a way that it can be turned. This adds a protractor-ruler feature to the compass' regular function.

When you use an Orienteering compass for determining map directions, the compass housing with its 360 degree markings becomes your protractor, the base plate with its straight sides your ruler. Since the compass needle plays no part in the job of using the Orienteering compass as a protractor-ruler, you can get along for this purpose with a needle-free Orienteering compass—and that's exactly what the training compass, which you will find in the envelope at the back of this book, is. Get out that training compass and learn the "slick-trick" method by which it will give you the map directions you seek.

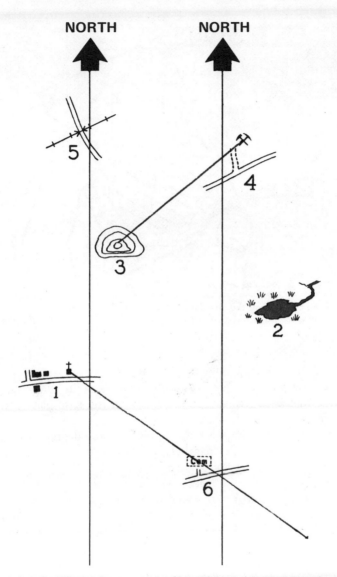

NORTH   NORTH

5

4

3

2

1

Con
6

Read instructions for this practice on page 40. Using the practicing protractor from the envelope in the back of this book, determine the directions between the points listed. Parallel lines are north-south meridians.

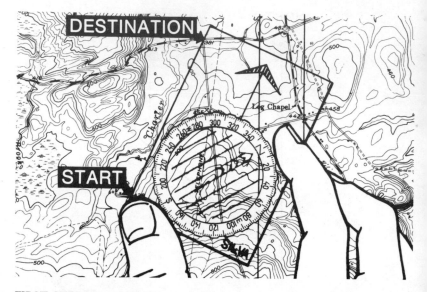

FIRST STEP in using the Orienteering compass as a protractor: place base plate on map in such a way that one edge touches both Start and Destination.

Place the training compass on the map in such a way that one edge of the base plate touches both your starting point and your destination, with the direction-of-travel arrow on the base plate pointing in the direction of the destination.

Now, turn the compass housing with its 360 degree markings until the orienting arrow lies parallel to the nearest north-south meridian line with the arrow point toward north.

Your compass is now "set." All you have to do to get the direction is to look at the degree marking on the rim of the compass housing where the direction line touches it. There is your direction in degrees. Easy? It sure is—with an Orienteering compass, or a "reasonable facsimile."

Orienteering Compass as Protractor—The training compass gives you the means for practice in using the compass as a protractor.

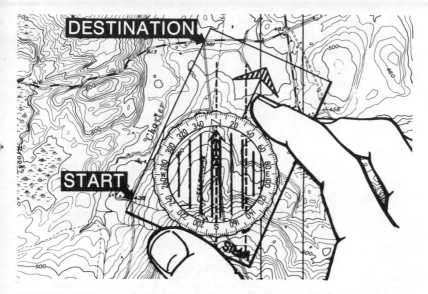

SECOND STEP in using the Orienteering compass as a protractor: turn housing with orienting arrow parallel to meridian. Read degrees over the black index pointer.

DIRECTION QUIZ   INDOOR PRACTICE

PURPOSE—Practice in determining degree directions on an actual map with the protractor-ruler of the Orienteering compass.

TEST YOURSELF—Open up the training map and take out the training compass from the envelope in the back of the book. Then find the directions in degrees between the following points:

1. From road-T in Glenburnie to top of Record Hill . . . . . .°
2. From Record Hill to crossroad south of BM 474 . . . . . . °
3. From crossroad south of BM 474 to Camp Adirondack . . . . .°
4. From Camp Adirondack to Log Chapel . . . . .°
5. From Log Chapel to Meadow Knoll Cemetery . . . . .°

(The correct answers are found on page 203.)

AS GAME—Provide each player with a training map and a training compass (from Orienteering Training Kit; see page 210). Then take each direction separately: "What is the direction in degrees from the road-T in Glenburnie to the top of Record Hill?" As soon as a player has determined the degrees, he holds up a hand. If correct within five degrees, he scores 20 points; if wrong, the next player has a chance to score. And so on, up to 100 points for all answers correct.

NOTE: If enough training maps are not available, Xerox the schematic map on page 41 and the list of degree readings on page 40, or mimeograph them and run off as many copies as you have players. Provide each player with a copy, a pencil, and a training compass. The player with the most correct answers in a ten-minute limit wins.

Distances

The scales in the bottom margin of your map give you the means for measuring distances on the map. These scales are usually given in four ways: (1) As a fraction—1:24,000 or 1:62,500; (2) as a ruler, known as a "bar scale," divided into miles and fractions of a mile; (3) as a ruler divided into thousands of feet; and (4) as a ruler divided into kilometers and fractions of kilometers.

On a map in the scale of 1:24,000 you know that 1 inch on any ordinary ruler represents 2,000 feet in the field. So you simply measure the number of inches and multiply by 2,000 to get the distance in feet. It is even simpler with a map in the scale 1:62,500 where the number of inches on the ruler gives you directly the number of miles on the ground.

Using the Map's Bar Scale

To use the bar scale on the map itself, mark off along the edge of a piece of paper the map distance between the two points for which you want to find the actual distance, then measure it against the bar scale in the bottom margin of the map. Or copy the bar scale on the map along the edge of a piece of paper and use this home-made ruler.

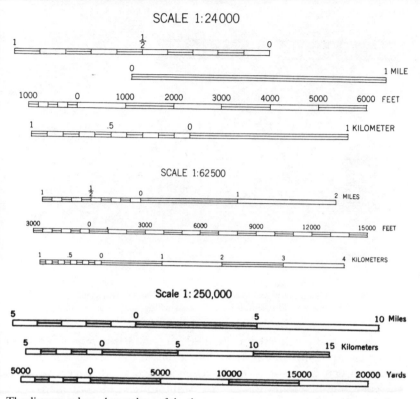

The distance rulers—bar scales—of the three most common map scales as shown in bottom margins of topographic maps. Copy to the edge of a piece of paper for measuring.

Orienteering Compass as Ruler

Even simpler: use the base plate of your Orienteering compass for measuring.

On some Orienteering compasses the base plate is marked in inches and millimeters, or with special scales. Others—such as your training compass—carry 1:24,000 and 1:62,500 scales for direct reading, as shown in the illustration above. One of the most popular compasses for Orienteering, the Silva® type 4s/22, comes with four interchangeable scales that can be slipped over the front edge of the base plate.

Some models of Orienteering compasses have distance rulers printed along two edges of the base plate. This simplifies the job of taking map measurements.

You can easily convert the front edge of the base plate of whatever Orienteering compass you have into a measuring device for the specific map you are using. Simply attach a piece of adhesive tape along the edge and copy onto this the bar scale, in feet, of your map.

Map Measurers

Another method for measuring distances on the map is to use a map measurer. This has a small wheel with which you follow on the map the road between your two points. The wheel is geared to a hand that turns around on a dial on which you can read the distance directly in the circle of figures for your particular map scale.

Distance Measuring—Practice distance measuring until you reach the point where you can look at your map and judge distances on it with fair accuracy.

PURPOSE—Practice in measuring distances on the map.

TEST YOURSELF—Transfer the bar scale on the training map to the edge of a piece of paper or a cardboard strip or use the practicing compass to find, on the training map, the crow-flight distances in feet between the following points:

1. From Log Chapel to Meadow Knoll Cemetery .... feet
2. From Meadow Knoll Cemetery to top of Hutton Hill .. feet
3. From top of Hutton Hill to Glenburnie .... feet
4. From Glenburnie to top of Record Hill .... feet
5. From top of Record Hill to Log Chapel .... feet

(You will find the answers on page 203.)

AS GAME—Each player has strip of paper or cardboard, pencil, and training map (in Orienteering Training Kit; see page 210). Leader asks, "What is the distance from Log Chapel to Meadow Knoll Cemetery?" First player with correct answer within fifty feet scores 20 points; 100 points for correct answers to all five questions.

Designations

Place Name Designations

Places and other map features are designated by name in various lettering styles.

Regular Roman (upright) type is used for places, boundary lines, and area names, while hydrographic names—water features—are in Italics (slanting type).

Hypsographic names—elevation features—are given in block letters, names of public works and special descriptive notes in leaning block letters (see illustration page 48).

Place, feature, boundary line, and area names

Richview, Union Sch, MADISON CO, C E D A R

Public works – Descriptive notes

ST LOUIS, ROAD, BELLE STREET, Tunnel - Golf Course, Radio Tower

Control data – Elevation figures – Contour numbers

Florey Knob, BM 1333, VABM 1217 – 5806 – 5500

Hypsographic names

Man Island, Burton Point, HEAD MOUNTAIN

Hydrographic names

Head Harbor, Wood River, NIAGARA RIVER

Place names are printed in varying lettering styles to make it easier to determine what
kind of landscape feature is meant.

Designation of Unmarked Locations

There will probably be many occasions when you'll need to indicate to someone else an exact location on the map not actually designated with a place name. The simplest way to do this is to make use
of the place name that is closest to the location.

Let's take an example: look at the training map in the back of the
book. Find the place name "Huckleberry Mtn" (Mountain). Then
locate the "Crossroads 1½ inches South-West of the letter 'H' in
Huckleberry Mtn" or we could write it simply "Crossroads 1½″ SW
H in **H**uckleberry Mtn"—underlining the letter we want to indicate.
All you have to do now is to measure from the bottom edge of the letter **H** 1½ inches (taken from the bar scale in the margin of the map, or
a regular ruler, or the ruler along the side of an Orienteering compass), in a south-westerly direction, and there is the crossroads. In
other words, find the place name, then the letter, then the distance,
and the direction.

The distances are measured from that part of the letter that is closest to the location you want to designate—that is, the bottom edge of
the letter if you want to measure in a general southerly direction, the
top edge if you are measuring north, left edge if west, right if east.

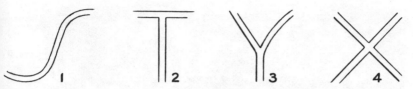

Terms designating road types spell STYX: 1. Road bend. 2. Road-T. 3. Road-Y or road fork. 4. Crossroads or Road-X.

Place Location Practice—In addition to the practice below, figure out for yourself how you would describe other locations in Orienteering "language."

FIND PLACES ON THE MAP   INDOOR PRACTICE

PURPOSE—To familiarize yourself with the method for designating unmarked locations on the map.

TEST YOURSELF—Locate the following places on the training map and write down on the dotted lines what they are:

1. 2″ S **R** in **R**ecord Hill ....
2. ³/₄″ E **e** in Chart**e**r Brook ....
3. 1⅝″ SE **U** in P**U**TNAM ....
4. 1³/₁₆″ WNW **H** in **H**utton Hill ....
5. 1⅛″ N **l** in Log Chape**l** ....
6. ⅝″ NW **M** in **M**eadow Knoll Cem ....
7. ¼″ N **k** in Suc**k**er Brook ....
8. 1½″ NE **l** in Record Hil**l** ....
9. ⅝″ W **L** in **L**og Chapel ....
10. ⅞″ S **l** in Huck**l**eberry Mtn ....

(You will find the correct answers on page 204.)

AS GAME—Copy the above list on blackboard, or give each player a mimeographed copy to fill out. Score 10 points for each map location correctly identified for a total of 100 points for all 10 places located.

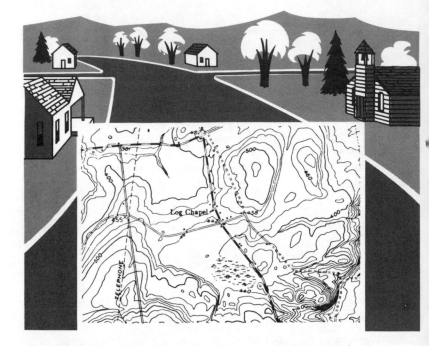

Compare the map with the landscape: Log Chapel is on the wrong side of the road, the road ahead bends in the wrong direction, etc. The map is obviously not "oriented."

TRAVELING BY MAP

Now that you know the features of a map, it is time to take a map walk. Decide on a place for starting your trip, lay out an appropriate route on the map, and try to follow it in the field.

Try an Imaginary Map "Walk" First

To give you the feeling of a typical map walk, unfold the training map and take an imaginary "walk" on it.

Let's say you decide to start from the crossroad south of Log

Compare the map with the landscape: Log Chapel is on the correct side of the road, the road ahead bends in the proper direction, etc. The map fits the landscape, is "oriented."

Chapel and take a "hike" that will bring you in counter-clockwise direction—east, north, west, south—along the route shown on page 52.

You arrive at Log Chapel then proceed south to the crossroads and are actually ready to start out. But in what direction? Do you go straight ahead, to the left, to the right, or straight backward?

Orienting the Map

The simplest way to know what direction to go on a map is by "orienting" the map. To "orient" a map means to turn it in such a way

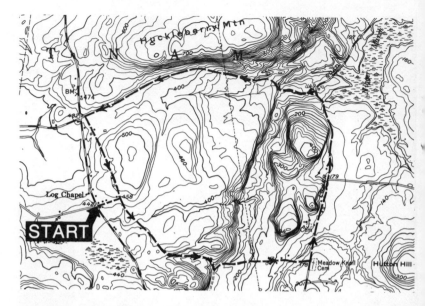

Follow an imaginary map "walk" (described on pages 50–51) on the training map in the back of this book. Begin at START and proceed in a counter-clockwise direction.

that north on the map fits north in the landscape, and that terrain features shown on the map, such as roads and rivers, are lined up with these features in the field.

So you inspect the map and your surroundings and twist the map around until the crossroads on it fit the actual crossroads at which you are standing, with Log Chapel in its right location.

You have "oriented" the map "by inspection."

The whole thing is simple now. The road to take is to the left of you. And to be doubly certain, you have an easy way of checking that it is the right one: about 800 feet ahead of you, you should strike a road-T.

Determining Distances

How do you know when you have walked 800 feet?

The best way of determining distances in the field is *by your step—*

For determining the length of your step, lay out a step course 200 feet long. Walk it twice, then divide the number of steps into the 400 feet covered.

or, even better, *by your double-step or pace*, counting off each time you put down the left foot—or right, if you prefer.

We have been doing it daily since Roman times.

Have you ever wondered why a mile contains the peculiar figure of 5,280 feet? For the reason that one thousand double-steps of the average Roman soldier at the time of the Caesars was that many times the length of the foot of that same soldier. The Latin for one thousand double-steps or paces, *mille passus*, was later abbreviated into our English "mile."

This will give you a clue to the length of your own double-step. It will be in the neighborhood of 5 feet—and for general uses that figure is close enough.

If you want to be more exact, measure the length of your double-step once and for all, and remember it.

To do this, lay out a step course. Drive a stake in the ground and measure out a distance of 200 feet with a tape measure. Place another

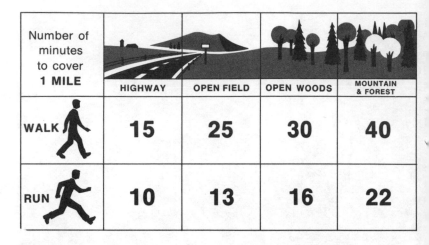

Number of minutes to cover 1 MILE	HIGHWAY	OPEN FIELD	OPEN WOODS	MOUNTAIN & FOREST
WALK	15	25	30	40
RUN	10	13	16	22

You can estimate the distance you have traveled by the number of minutes elapsed. Various speeds and terrains influence the time needed to cover 1 mile.

stake here. Then walk from stake to stake and back again, counting your double-steps. Divide the complete length covered—400 feet—by the number of double-steps taken. This will give you the length of your average pace. If you covered it in 80 double-steps, your average double-step is 5 feet. If you used 90 double-steps, each double-step is close to 4½ feet.

Another way of determining the distance you have covered is *by time elapsed*. This is shown schematically in the drawing on this page. The times given here are for each mile covered—15 minutes, for instance, for walking one mile along a good road, 25 minutes along a trail, and so on.

The Importance of a Date

You start walking toward the road-T, but before you reach it you are puzzled by a road leading off to the right. It shouldn't be there—it isn't on the map.

What has happened? Simply this: your map, as indicated on the frame of it, was last revised in 1950—and much can have happened

Topography from aerial photographs by multiplex methods
Aerial photographs taken 1942. Field check 1949-1950

Polyconic projection. 1927 North American datum
10,000-foot grids based on New York coordinate system,
east zone, and Vermont coordinate system

EDITION OF
1950

Dates are important. Your map was correct when last revised—but don't be surprised if
changes have occurred—especially if you use an old edition.

since 1950, and apparently did. What happened in this particular in-stance was that a building lot was sold, a house was put up, and a road was constructed leading into it from the road on which you are standing.

Which only shows how important it is to be aware of the last revision date of the map, and of the possible changes that can have taken place: a secondary road may have been improved into a primary road; a marsh may have been drained for farm land or may have been turned into a pond; a forest may have been cut down; or a wood lot may have been planted.

So after you have set your mind at ease regarding this un-mapped road, you proceed—and, sure enough, you hit the road-T exactly at 800 feet.

Along the Road

At the road-T you "orient" your map again and turn south-eastward along the right "arm" of the top line of the T. Second-growth woods are all around you on rather level land—as it should be according to the map since the contour lines are far apart. You cross an overgrown brook and soon after the improved road turns into an unimproved one. The map is right again—the thin parallel lines that indicate the type road become broken lines.

The road swings toward the east and starts dropping, then toward the south with a steeper drop. You have reached the road-Y, coming in on the left "arm." In the crotch of the Y, you change direction and go north-eastward along the Y's right "arm." You are in flat country again, with a meandering brook and a small lake on your right. The unimproved road gets better and soon you find yourself at the road-T opposite Meadow Knoll Cemetery—a typical country graveyard with a number of old headstones.

You orient your map again, then turn left, northward on the high-way. For greater safety, you walk on the left side of the road, facing the oncoming traffic.

According to schedule, you pass an old country church at your left and a side road at your right. Ahead of you, to the left, rises a steep tree-clad cliff. How steep is it? Plenty steep—just look at those con-tour lines; they are right on top of each other. How high? Locate the number 179 on the map at the point where the side road strikes the highway—that's the elevation of that particular point. Now "crawl" up the cliff: you cross the light 180-foot contour line and the heavier 200-foot line, then several light lines, the heavy 300-foot con-tour, more light lines, and then the heavy 400-foot contour line. The 400-foot line is closed to indicate the top of the hill, but there is another closed line within it—the 420-foot contour.

You figure the view from that hill should be pretty good and decide to climb it. You wouldn't want to climb the cliff wall, but the map tells you that the hill slopes up more easily from the north. So you walk up the road "a piece"—about 2,000 feet beyond the side road—and climb the hill from there. You were right—the view is spectacular over the valley, over fertile fields and lush green marshes toward dis-tant hills.

Down, and northward again along the road until it swings north-east. There should be an unimproved road to the left. If that's the road, it surely *is* unimproved. But it must be right—there's a farm house and a couple of barns close by in exactly the same relative location to each other as the symbols on the map. You take a chance on the road and soon discover that it is correct enough, for the cliff wall of Huckle-berry Mountain rises high on your right as you hike along the lane.

Eventually the road improves and you can see cars whizzing by on the main road that lies ahead. But just before you strike the main road, you turn left on an unimproved road to keep away from main road traffic and shortly afterwards arrive at a familiar point—the road-T you passed on the out-trip. A few feet more along the road to the right—the same 800 feet that formed the first leg of your

Whenever you reach a prominent landmark or a turn in your route, take time to orient your map. You will then always know exactly where you are.

journey—and you are back at your starting point, the crossroads south of Log Chapel.

Now for an Actual Outdoor Walk by Map

Your map walk was a fairly simple one—especially since you took it reading these pages without actually walking it.

In the Landmark Hunt project you learn to orient a map and to locate important landscape features on it. Pointers can be made from scrap wood.

Now get out the map of your home territory, plan a trip on it, and take an actual walk by map through your own countryside.

Don't be too ambitious the first couple of times. A walk of four to five miles should give you a good idea of the use of a map.

Outdoor Map Practice—As soon as possible, get out in the field and make use of the knowledge you have just gained. *Indoor practice* is all right, but *outdoor use* is the "proof of the pudding."

LANDMARK HUNT   OUTDOOR PRACTICE

PURPOSE—Training in orienting a map and in locating landmarks.

GROUP PROJECT—Bring the group to a high station point of good visibility where a number of different landmarks can be seen. Provide each player or buddy team with a topographic map of the area, a pencil, and a list of 10 landmarks to be located on the map, such as:

1. Indicate on your map, by drawing a circle around it, the point where you are now standing.
2. Circle church approximately NW of here.
3. Circle crossroads approximately S of here.
4. Circle dam approximately ESE of here.

And so on, for 10 landmarks.

Set a certain time for finishing the project, such as twenty minutes. Score 10 points for each landmark correctly found and circled on the map, up to 100 points for all ten.

NOTE: Instead of using a list of landmarks, which at best can only be approximate, and also to add more interest, put up a number of markers in a circle about 30 feet in diameter, each marker pointing to a different landmark. These markers may be made of strips of wood, 1″ x 2″ x 10″, using nails to act as sights. One end of each marker is pointed, the other end carries a strip of cardboard with a description of the landmark to which the marker points—such as "Church," "Bridge," and so on. The markers are fastened at eye level to uprights of 1″ x 1″ wood, or 1″ dowel sticks, with wing nuts. Players move clockwise from marker to marker.

MAP POINT WALK   OUTDOOR PRACTICE

PURPOSE—Practice in following a route and locating on the map landmarks found on the way. Map Point Walk is an especially good preliminary project for promoting a general interest in Orienteering. Almost anybody can participate since little skill is required and because there is no chance of anyone's getting lost. Also, any number of people may participate, from a small group to a very large one.

GROUP PROJECT—On a map, lay out an appropriate route of two to three miles leading through a number of easily definable landmarks. Then go over the route in the field and mark it by tying colored streamers (one-inch-wide strips of red crepe paper or plastic) to trees, posts, or sticks at such distances that the next marker along the route can readily be seen from the preceding one. Hang a much wider streamer or a regular Orienteering marker (see page 192) and place a north-pointing arrow marker at each of the main landmarks on the route to assist the participants in orienting their maps.

Send out the participants at two-minute intervals, each provided with a map and a pencil. The object is to follow the marked route and indicate on the map, by circling it, each of the color-streamered landmarks.

The scoring may be done on a time basis, the person with the lowest number of minutes winning, providing his landmark indications are correct. If incorrect, he may be penalized by having five minutes added to his time for each error in marking.

NOTE: In case of a large group participating (twenty or more) it will prove advantageous to station a judge at each of the landmarks and have him score the participants for his specific location.

MAP POINT REPORTING   OUTDOOR PRACTICE

PURPOSE—Combining map reading and observation to provide greater enjoyment of traveling by map.

GROUP PROJECT—On a map, locate six to ten clearly indicated landmarks over a 2- to 4-mile route. Then hike to each landmark and develop a suitable question regarding objects found there or terrain features seen from that spot—such as what types of trees are growing there, what large buildings may be seen, and so on. Decide on an appropriate scoring value for each correct answer. Start the participants at two-minute intervals, each with a map, a pencil, and a report card describing the location of each landmark, the task to be accomplished, and the score value for correct answers. The object is to score the maximum number of points within a three-hour time

In the Map Point Walk follow a route marked by colored streamers. The object is to locate and mark on your map certain landmarks passed en route.

In Map Point Reporting each participant tries to find half a dozen or more landmarks and copies a code letter or performs a project at each landmark.

limit. The participant decides for himself in what order to visit the landmarks and how many of them he feels he can manage to cover. He may decide, for instance, to locate first the landmarks that have the highest score value and then try to cover as many of the others as possible within the time limit. The finished report card is turned in to the judge at the finishing point and the score computed.

PART II

Fun with Compass Alone

A great number of years ago—estimates say around 2500 B.C.—some clever Chinese discovered that a piece of a certain ore, floated on water on a piece of wood, would turn until one end of it pointed in the general direction from which the sun shone half way between sunrise and sunset—the direction he knew as south, or its Chinese equivalent. And if one end of the floating ore pointed south, the other end obviously pointed north.

Out of that discovery emerged the compass needle—a strip of magnetized steel balanced on a pivot, free to swing in any direction.

When left to itself, this needle eventually comes to rest with one end pointing north. On commercial compasses this end is clearly indicated as the north end. It is either painted (black or red) or stamped with the initial N, or both, or formed in the shape of an arrow.

The Compass Needle Points Magnetic North

The force that attracts this magnetized needle is the magnetism of the earth. The whole earth is like a tremendous magnet, with one "end" in the north, the other in the south. The north "end" is the magnetic North Pole toward which the north end of the compass needle points when at rest.

If you belong to the kind of people who like things to be uncomplicated, you would want to have the magnetic North Pole coincide with the true or geographic North Pole. Unfortunately, it doesn't. The magnetic North Pole which attracts the compass needle is located about 1,400 miles south of the true North Pole near an island—Bathurst Island—off the northern coast of Canada.

That means in Orienteering you will have two north directions to deal with—true north as it is shown on your map, and magnetic north as you find it with the help of the compass needle. Sooner or later you'll need to make these two norths jibe—but for the time being we'll concern ourselves with the north the compass needle gives.

Development of the Compass

After the invention of the compass needle, someone got the bright idea of protecting it by enclosing it in a metal case. In the beginning this was a simple air-filled brass housing in which the needle swung around freely, suspended on a point—*air compasses* or *standard compasses*.

The next step was to find a way of breaking the swinging of the magnetic needle so that it would come to rest quickly. Different devices have been developed for this purpose. In some modern compasses the magnetized needle swings in a copper-lined housing and in its swinging sets up electric currents which bring the needle to a fast halt—the so-called *induction-dampened compasses*. The most effective method, used in most modern compasses, is to fill the housing with a

The history of the compass goes back more than 800 years. Records show that the magnetized compass needle was used by Chinese sailors around the year 1100 A.D., by Arabian merchants around 1220 A.D., by Scandinavian Vikings in 1250 A.D.

Early Chinese compasses (sample at right) were made of lacquer ware, painted with figures and symbols.

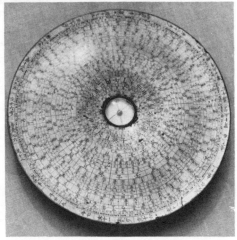

Diptych compasses (left) were made in Europe from ivory by such Nurenberg craftsmen as Hans Ducher (1576) and Hans Troschel (1624).

Octagonal-shaped sundial compass in silver (right) was wrought in Paris by Claude Langlois around 1725.

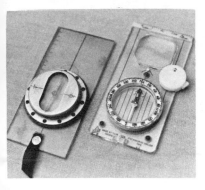

The Silva compass has developed from the part-metal prototype of the 1930s into the modern plastic-type compass that has turned Orienteering into a world-wide sport.

liquid that slows down the jiggling of the needle and brings it to rest quickly—*liquid-filled compasses.*

Until comparatively recently the compass housing was marked with the thirty-two points of the mariner's compass. Then some other imaginative person suggested the 360 degrees of a full circle. Because of this, the compass today shows 360 different directions or "bearings" instead of just the thirty-two of the old-fashioned "compass rose."

And finally, the conventional "watch-case" compass was improved into the modern *Orienteering compass* in which the compass housing revolves on a transparent base plate that acts as protractor and direction finder. This type of compass, invented in Sweden in the early 1930s, has taken the guesswork out of direction finding and has made the use of map and compass easy and accurate.

Compass Point Practice—In the following pages there will be many references to the sixteen most commonly used traditional compass

The marine compasses of today carry not only the old compass direction designations, but also the 360° of a circle.

directions. Before proceeding, familiarize yourself thoroughly with these compass directions.

COMPASS ROSE QUIZ   INDOOR PRACTICE

PURPOSE—To learn sixteen of the traditional compass directions.

TEST YOURSELF—Study the compass rose on page 66, then quickly mark the sixteen points on the figure on the bottom of this page.

AS GAME—Provide each player with a copy of the figure on this page. On the signal "Go" each player attempts to fill in the names of the sixteen compass directions. The player filling in the figure correctly in the shortest time wins.

COMPASS FACING   INDOOR PRACTICE

PURPOSE—Quick review of the sixteen main compass directions.

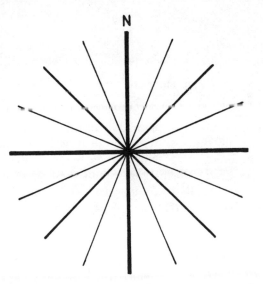

Study the compass rose on the preceding page, then get out your pencil and write down the names of the sixteen traditional compass points.

Compass Facing is a simple game for practice in memorizing the main compass directions. It can be played indoors as well as out-of-doors.

TEST YOURSELF—Stand in the middle of the room facing one of the walls. Designate the spot on the wall directly in front of you as North. Now quickly face North, then South, West, East, North-West, South-East, North-East, South-West, North-North-East, South-South-West, East, South-East, West-North-West, South-South-East, West-South-West, East-North-East, North-North-West.

AS GAME—Participants line up in open lines, an arm's length apart sideways and front-and-back. One wall of the room is designated North. On the signal "North-East GO!" all turn to face what they believe to be North-East; then on the command "Freeze!" stand motionless. Those who are facing incorrectly go out of the game. Continue until only one player is left—the "champeen." OR let those who face correctly go out of the game to give more training to those who need more practice.

TRAVELING BY COMPASS ALONE

The three main purposes for which you can use the compass alone—without the additional help of a map—are these:

1. Finding directions—"bearings"—from a location.
2. Following a direction—a "bearing"—from a location.
3. Returning to your original location.

Using the Conventional Compass

Let us say that your tool is the conventional compass—a magnetized needle suspended on a point in a compass housing marked in 360 degrees.

Finding Directions with the Conventional Compass

Let us assume that you are standing on some elevated spot or open ground and want to know the directions or "bearings" to various landmarks around you—a distant hilltop, a church spire, a water tower, or what-have-you.

Face squarely the landmark for which you want to determine a bearing, and hold your compass steady in front of you in one hand. With the other hand, slowly turn the compass housing until the north part of the compass needle rests over the north marking of the compass housing.

Now sight across the center of the compass and read the number of degrees on the compass housing directly opposite your face.

There you have the direction toward the landmark expressed in degrees.

It is obvious that this kind of sighting and reading will give you a very crude specification that may vary a number of degrees in either direction. That is why the better compasses of the watch-case type are provided with a sighting device containing a lens ("lensatic" compass) or a prism ("prismatic" compass) through which the reading is done. But those devices increase the cost substantially without materially adding to the usefulness of the compass.

Following a Direction with the Conventional Compass

Let's say that you want to explore the distant hilltop you can see from where you are standing and decide to reach it by traveling cross-country through the landscape that lies before you.

You determine the bearing to your destination by the method described in the preceding paragraphs and find it to be, say, 140°. *Remember that number.* Or even better, jot it down—for sooner or later you will start wondering whether you remember it correctly or not.

Start walking toward your destination. In the beginning it is easy—you can see it right there ahead of you. But suddenly it disappears! You have been walking down a slope and the trees in front of you block off the view. This is where you start "flying blind"—using the compass only.

The conventional compass is generally of the "watchcase" type. The compass is oriented when the north part of the needle lies over the north arrow on the bottom of the case.

The direction you have to travel by compass is 140°. Hold the compass in the palm of your hand with the compass housing turned in such a way that the 140° marking is on the far side of the compass center. Rotate your whole body until you have the compass "oriented"—that is, until the north part of the compass needle comes to rest pointing at the 360° N marking of the compass housing.

Now sight across the center of the compass and through the 140° marking of the compass housing. Notice some landmark in that direction—a large rock, a prominent tree—and walk to this landmark. Here, take the same bearing toward another landmark—and continue in this way until you reach your destination.

Returning to Original Location

After you have had your fill of exploring around your destination, you are ready for the return journey.

You traveled out in the direction of 140°. To determine the bearing of your return direction—your "back bearing"—add 180° (the number of degrees of a half-circle) and get for your result 320°. (If the number of degrees of your original direction had been larger than 180° you would have *subtracted* 180° from it instead of adding them.)

Again, remember carefully the number of degrees—320°—of your return journey. As before, jot it down just to be sure. Then set out for home:

Use your compass as before, holding it in the palm of your hand with the 320° marking on the far side of the compass center. Turn your body until the compass is oriented with the north point of the compass needle pointing to the north marking of the compass case and sight toward the first landmark of your return journey.

If you have been careful in reading your directions and in sighting, you should have no trouble finding your way back safely.

Using the Modern Orienteering Compass

You will have a much easier time with compass traveling if, instead of using the conventional compass, you use a modern Orienteering compass—the Polaris®, the Explorer III, the Voyager, the Huntsman®, or some other compass based on the Silva® System (see illustrations page 214).

The modern Orienteering compass gives you directions directly, without the intermediate step of having to figure out and to check degree numbers. It makes it unnecessary to keep degree numbers in your head. It gives you the return direction without the necessity of adding or subtracting, thus eliminating the possibility of making a mistake in figuring that may have dire consequences. And when used with a map, the modern Orienteering compass combines compass, protractor, and ruler in a single tool.

The Parts of the Orienteering Compass

The modern Orienteering compass consists of three basic parts: magnetic needle, a revolving compass housing, and a transparent base plate—each part with its own special function, but all three working together to make the Orienteering compass an efficient and highly practical instrument.

The *magnetic needle* of the Orienteering compass is suspended on a needle-sharp point around which it swings freely on a sapphire bearing. The north end of the needle is painted red—on some models it is also marked with a luminous band.

The rim of the *compass housing* is marked with the initials of the four "cardinal points"—North, East, South, and West—and is divided into degree lines. Each space between the lines on the housing represents two degrees. Every twentieth degree line is marked by a number—from 20 to 360. The transparent inside bottom of the compass housing is provided with an arrow that points directly to the housing's 360° N marking. This arrow is the "orienting arrow." The compass is "oriented"—that is, turned so that the north marking of the compass points toward the magnetic North Pole—whenever the red north end of the magnetic needle lies over the orienting arrow, pointing toward the letter N on the rim of the housing. In the bottom of the compass housing are engraved several lines which run parallel with the orienting arrow—these lines are the compass' orienting lines.

The compass housing is attached to a rectangular transparent *base plate* in such a way that it can be turned easily. A line to show direc-

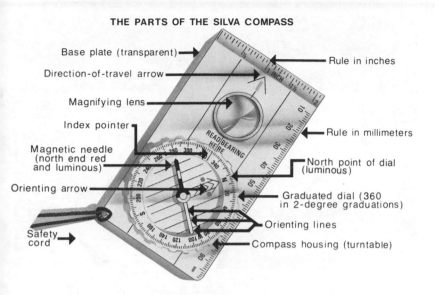

THE PARTS OF THE SILVA COMPASS

Base plate (transparent)

Direction-of-travel arrow

Magnifying lens

Index pointer

Magnetic needle
(north end red
and luminous)

Orienting arrow

Safety
cord

Rule in inches

Rule in millimeters

North point of dial
(luminous)

Graduated dial (360
in 2-degree graduations)

Orienting lines

Compass housing (turntable)

READ BEARING
HERE

The parts of a modern Orienteering compass.

tion is engraved in this base plate. It runs from the rim of the compass housing to the front edge of the plate where it spreads into an arrow—called the direction-of-travel arrow. The raised part of the base plate (on which the compass housing moves) has a black index pointer on a white background to show at what degree number the compass housing is set. The side edges of the base plate are parallel to the direction-of-travel arrow line.

The side edge and the front edge of the base plate have markings for measuring—on some models inches and millimeters, on others the more common map scales. Still other Orienteering compasses come with exchangeable scales for use with maps of different scales.

Finding Bearings with the Orienteering Compass

Finding a bearing with the Orienteering compass is a simple matter: face squarely a distant point or landmark. Hold the Orienteering

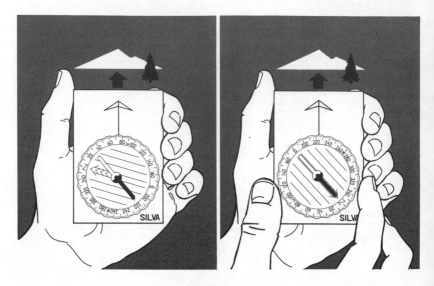

To find a direction with the Orienteering compass, point the direction-of-travel arrow to a landmark and turn the housing until the needle lies over the orienting arrow. The bearing to the hill is 225°.

compass level at waist height or a little higher with the direction-of-travel arrow pointing straight ahead.

Orient your compass by turning the compass housing without moving the base plate until the compass needle lies over the orienting arrow on the inside bottom of the compass housing, with its north part pointing to the letter N.

Read the bearing—the degrees of the direction—on the rim of the compass housing at the spot where the black index pointer shows it to be.

It is as easy as that with an Orienteering compass—no sighting over the center and outside rim and no chance of an incorrect reading as with the ordinary compass.

Direction Finding Practice—Before going outdoors become thoroughly familiar with the use of the compass through indoor practice. Then transfer the practice to a suitable location in the field.

PURPOSE—Learning the use of the Orienteering compass for taking direction bearings.

TEST YOURSELF—Stand in the middle of the room. With the Orienteering compass determine 10 different directions by the method described on pages 73–74. Examples: to door handle; nearest leg of table; right-hand edge of window; picture on wall—and so on.

AS GROUP GAME—Prepare for the game by chalking on the floor as many numbers as there are players, and by taping the same number of numbered cards on a wall. Then determine the degree readings from each number on the floor to the corresponding number on the wall and make a list of them. Each player should have an Orienteering compass, a pencil, and a piece of paper. The game starts with each participant taking a position over a number on the floor. On the signal "Go" each player takes the degree reading to the card that bears the same number he is standing on and writes down that number and the degree bearing on his paper. On signal "Change" all players move up—player No. 1 to the No. 2 marking on the floor, player No. 2 to the No. 3 marking, and so on. When in position, another "Go" signal is given and each player takes his next reading toward the card that bears the number on which he is now standing. And so on for five or more readings. The player with the most correct readings within 10 degrees wins.

AS RELAY GAME—Instead of as many chalk numbers as players, only one chalk number is written on the floor for each team. On the walls fasten as many numbered cards as there are players in each relay team. Each team has one Orienteering compass. On the signal "Go!" the first player of each relay team runs to his team mark on the floor and takes a reading to the card numbered "1." He returns and touches off the second player who runs up and takes a reading to card "2"—and so on. The fastest team with the most correct readings wins.

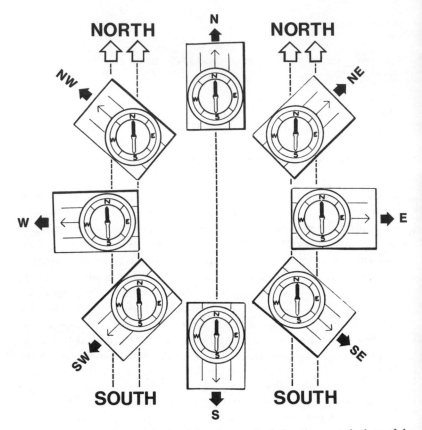

To go in any of the four cardinal and four intercardinal directions, set the base of the direction line at the direction desired, orient the compass, and follow the direction-of-travel arrow.

FIND DIRECTIONS OUTDOORS · · · · · · · · · · · · · · OUTDOOR PRACTICE

PURPOSE—Complete familiarity with the use of the Orienteering compass for finding bearings in the field

TEST YOURSELF—Proceed to a location from which a dozen or more prominent landmarks may be seen. With the Orienteering compass, determine the compass direction to each of them by the method described on pages 73–74.

GROUP PROJECT—At a high station point of good visibility set up a number of markers as described on page 59, each marker pointing to a prominent landmark. Bring the group to the station and provide each player with an Orienteering compass, pencil, and paper. Have each player move clockwise from marker to marker and determine the compass direction toward each of the landmarks to which the markers point. Set a time limit for finishing the project—such as 20 minutes. Score 10 points for each compass direction correct to within 5 degrees.

Following a Bearing with the Orienteering Compass

Let's say you're standing somewhere out in the field and have made up your mind to proceed cross-country to a hilltop in the distance.

Set your Orienteering compass for the direction in which the hill-

To go in a certain direction, set the degree number over the index pointer, point the direction-of-travel arrow straight ahead of you, orient the compass, and proceed.

top lies by holding your compass with the direction-of-travel arrow pointing toward your destination. Turn the compass housing until the red north part of the compass needle points to the letter N on the rim of the housing. Proceed straight ahead in the direction the direction-of-travel arrow points.

If you lose sight of the distant hilltop, hold the compass in front of you, orient it, and sight toward some close-by landmark—rock or tree—in the direction in which the arrow points. Walk to that, then take a similar reading to another landmark—and so on until you reach the destination. Only watch this: do not twist the compass housing once you have set the compass for your direction.

What about compass degrees? What about figures to remember? You can forget about compass degrees and figures when you use the Orienteering compass—that's one of its great advantages. Your compass is already set—there's nothing to remember. Just orient it and proceed.

Returning to Original Location

You have reached your destination then decide to return home. How?

Your Orienteering compass is already set for your return journey!

When you went out, you held the compass with the direction-of-travel arrow at the front of the base plate pointing *away from you* toward your destination. Obviously, then, the back of the base plate was in the opposite direction, pointing backward toward the spot from which you set out.

Make use of this fact for your return trip.

Hold the compass level in the usual manner, but with the direction-of-travel arrow pointing *toward you* instead of away from you. Orient the compass by turning your whole body—DO NOT TOUCH THE COMPASS HOUSING—until the north end of the needle points to the N of the compass housing. Raise your eyes and locate a landmark in front of you. Walk to this landmark. Orient the compass again, pick another landmark ahead of you—and so on until you have returned to your original location.

No degree figures to remember. No subtraction or addition with

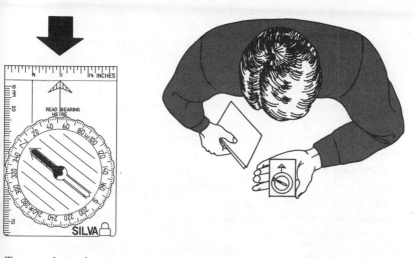

To return home do not reset the compass. Instead, point the direction-of-travel arrow toward you, orient the compass, and walk against the direction-of-travel arrow.

possible errors in calculation. Your Orienteering compass is set— simply use it backward.

Direction Following Practice—For precision compass work, it is important to be able to follow a compass bearing without reference to any landscape feature—figuratively "blindfolded." For practice, use the equivalent of a blindfold.

Blindfold Compass Walk   Outdoor Practice

PURPOSE—Learning to follow a compass bearing with precision.

TEST YOURSELF—Go to an open field and place a stake in the ground. Set your Orienteering compass at any bearing you desire. Place a large paper bag over your head, folding its edge so that you can see the compass held at waist height but cannot see ahead. Turn around three times, then orient the compass and walk 50 steps in the direction set on it. Stop. Turn the compass for the return journey—that is, with the direction-of-travel arrow pointing toward you. Walk back toward the stake 45 steps. Stop. You should be within less than 10 steps of the stake.

GROUP PROJECT—Set up half as many numbered stakes as there are players, 5 feet apart in a north-south line. Divide the players into two teams and place a player from each team at each stake. Have the players of one team set their compasses at bearings between 45° and 115°, the players of the other team between 225° and 315°. Each player, bag over head and compass in hand, turns around three times, follows his compass bearing for 50 steps, then turns and follows the back bearing for 45 steps. Only players winding up within 10 steps of their stakes score. The team with the most scorers wins.

TRAVELING BY COMPASS

So far, your compass work has been rudimentary practice. It is time for you to get into the field for some more comprehensive compass work. So get out there with your Orienteering compass and test your compass skill.

A Three-Legged Compass Walk

Try a simple compass walk first over a short distance.

Ready to gamble a quarter on your compass skill? No? Well, then make it a nickel. Place a nickel on the ground between your feet. Set the compass for an arbitrary direction between 0 and 120° by twisting the compass housing until the black index pointer on the rim is at the degree number you have decided on. What'll it be—40°? Fine. The compass is now set for traveling in the direction of 40°.

Hold the compass level with the direction-of-travel arrow straight ahead. Move your body until the compass needle is oriented—that is, until the north part of the needle points to the N of the compass housing. Look up and decide on a landmark straight ahead of you in the 40° direction. Walk straight toward that landmark

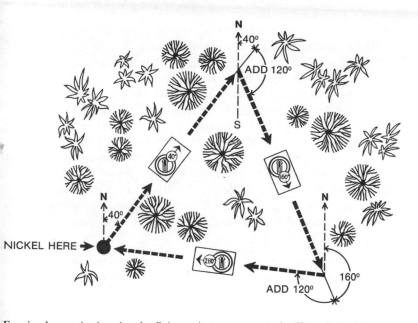

NICKEL HERE ➤

For simple practice in using the Orienteering compass try the Three-Legged Compass Walk. Place a marker and add 120° to each setting from the original.

without looking at your compass—for 40 steps, which is around 100 feet. Stop.

Look at your compass again. Add 120° to your original 40°—making it 160°. Reset your compass housing so that the index pointer now is at the 160° marking. Again, hold the compass flat before you, direction-of-travel arrow pointing straight ahead. Move your whole body until the compass needle lies over the orienting arrow in the housing, with the north part pointing to N. Again, look up, pick a landmark in the direction of 160°, and walk toward it 40 steps. Stop.

Again, add 120° to your setting of 160°—making it 280°. Reset your compass, determine the direction to walk, and take 40 steps in the direction toward which the direction-of-travel arrow points. Stop. Bend down and pick up your nickel! The nickel should be right at your feet if your compass readings and your walking were exact.

How come? Look at the diagram above. You have been walking

the three sides of an equilateral triangle. When you finish you should be right back at your starting point.

Try this same stunt a couple of times, each time starting out with a degree setting somewhere between 0 and 120°.

Now that you have the idea you'll realize that you don't really need to stick to a starting direction between 0 and 120°. That was done for the sake of simplicity. You can pick any number of degrees that suits you. You then have to remember that any time in your adding that you arrive at a figure larger than 360°, you must *subtract* 360° from it to get your next direction. Let's take an example: your first direction is 225°. Your second is 225° plus 120°, or 345°. Your third would then be 345° plus 120°, or 465°. There is no such figure on your compass—so you subtract 360° and get 105°, your correct third direction.

Outdoor Direction Practice—When you can quickly use your Orienteering compass, set out on simple outdoor compass practices.

SILVER DOLLAR HUNT   OUTDOOR PRACTICE

PURPOSE—Practice in taking degree bearings and following them.

GROUP PROJECT—The Silver Dollar Hunt is the Three-Legged Compass Walk described on pages 80–81 turned into a project for a small or medium-sized group—such as a Scout patrol.

Make up as many "silver dollars" (2–3-inch lids cut from tin cans) as there are participants, and a number of instruction cards with distances and directions, such as:

> "40 steps 90°—40 steps 210°—40 steps 330°"
> "50 steps 45°—50 steps 165°—50 steps 285°"
> "45 steps 18°—45 steps 138°—45 steps 258°"

(Notice that on the same card all the distances are alike and that the directions start with a degree bearing of less than 120° to which are added first 120°, then another 120°—for the explanation see page 82.) Scatter the participants over a field with fairly tall grass, or in a wooded terrain with a fair amount of underbrush. Place a "silver dollar" at the feet of each player. On a signal, each player takes the first bearing and walks the first distance, then stops. When all have stopped, give the next signal. Each takes the second bearing indicated on his card, walks the second distance, stops. On the third signal, all walk their third distance and stop. On the fourth and last signal, all bend down and pick up the "silver dollar"—which should be lying at their feet, or at least within sight, if the compass walking has been done correctly. Each player who can pick up his "silver dollar" scores 100 points.

SCHOOLYARD COMPASS GAME   OUTDOOR PRACTICE

PURPOSE—Practice in setting the compass for degree bearings and following them with precision. (Designed by Allan Foster.)

GROUP PROJECT—The course for this game can be set up in a school-yard, in a park, or in Scout camp. The course consists of eight

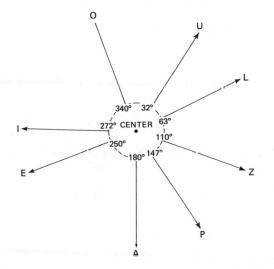

The course for the Schoolyard Compass Game consists of eight stakes placed at the same distance but at different compass bearings from a center stake.

marked stakes set up in a large circle. The stakes are marked I, O, U, L, Z, E, A, and P. For laying out the course you also need an unmarked center stake, a string 50 feet long or longer, and an Orienteering compass.

To lay out the course place the unmarked stake in the center of the area you have chosen for the game. Attach the measuring string to this center stake. Starting from the center stake each time, set the compass bearing as indicated in the illustration; stretch out the measuring string along this bearing and place the respective marked stake at the end of the string. The success of the game depends on the careful positioning of these markers.

To play the game each participant is provided with an Orienteering compass, a pencil, and an instruction card. The card tells him at what marked stake to start and directs him to follow five compass bearings from marker to marker around the course. You will find instructions below for the cards for ten players. If your group is larger, either run the participants in several sections or secure printed instruction cards for 99 players from the Orienteering Services (for addresses, see page 210).

1. Start at stake marked A
Proceed 305, 29, 100, 162, 221
Markers reached: . . . .

2. Start at stake marked E
Proceed 358, 68, 140, 198, 252
Markers reached: . . . .

3. Start at stake marked I
Proceed 42, 112, 178, 236, 305
Markers reached: . . . .

4. Start at stake marked O
Proceed 100, 162, 221, 287, 358
Markers reached: . . . .

5. Start at stake marked U
Proceed 140, 198, 252, 320, 42
Markers reached: . . . .

6. Start at stake marked L
Proceed 178, 236, 305, 29, 100
Markers reached: . . . .

7. Start at stake marked Z
Proceed 221, 287, 358, 68, 140
Markers reached: . . . .

8. Start at stake marked P
Proceed 252, 320, 42, 112, 178
Markers reached: . . . .

9. Start at stake marked A
Proceed 320, 68, 162, 236, 305
Markers reached: . . . .

10. Start at stake marked E
Proceed 29. 112, 198, 287, 358
Markers reached: . . . .

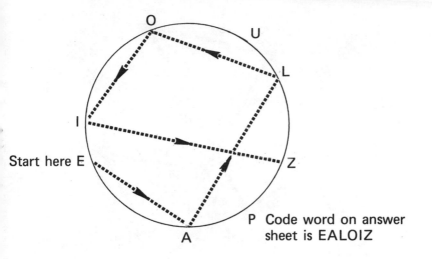

Start here E

P Code word on answer
sheet is EALOIZ

A player in the Schoolyard Compass Game is told to start at stake E and to proceed
125, 26, 292, 222, 106. His answering code word would be EALOIZ.

When ready to start, each participant goes to the marker which has
the letter that corresponds to the starting point of his instruction
card and proceeds according to instructions. The player copies
down on his card the letter on each marker along his route. When
he has finished, he turns his card over to the Judge. The six letter
code word produced, beginning with starting-stake letter, is then
checked against the correct code word as found on page 204.

MINI-ORIENTEERING WALK   OUTDOOR PRACTICE

PURPOSE—The Mini-Orienteering Compass Walk covers an area of
only a few hundred yards yet gives excellent training in walking
cross-country by compass.

GROUP PROJECT—The course for this game is laid in wooded territory by attaching a series of markers to the trees, each marker with

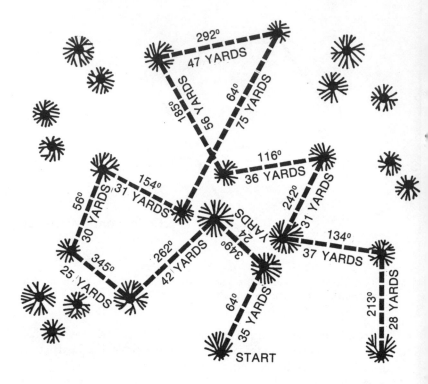

A typical course for a Mini-Orienteering Walk. It can be arranged in a school playground area, at a Scout camp site, or in a local park.

its own number and with the direction and distance to the next post.

The course is most simply laid by two people working together, each with a marking pencil. Tack marker No. 1 on a tree and decide on a certain compass bearing. Write the degree number on the marker, then, leaving your helper at Post No. 1, proceed in that direction, measuring the distance by your steps, until you reach another tree that can appropriately become Post No. 2. Yell the distance to your helper waiting at Post No. 1, who thereupon writes this distance on the No. 1 marker and joins you at Post No. 2. In the meantime, you have put up the Post No. 2 marker—preferably

Mini-Orienteering Walk provides training in walking cross-country by compass. Very little space is required for putting up an effective course.

To follow degree specified, set the number over the index pointer . . .

. . . point direction-of-travel arrow ahead, orient compass, proceed.

on the back of the tree so that it cannot be seen as you approach it—and have written on it a new bearing. Follow this bearing until you decide on the location of Post No. 3. And so on, for about a dozen posts.

The participants are started at two-minute intervals and each of them is provided with an Orienteering compass. Fastest time around the course wins.

COMPASS COMPETITION   OUTDOOR PRACTICE

PURPOSE—Training in following compass bearings and measuring distances by walking. This type of compass competition is particularly suited for school grounds and camp sites. The course can be set up quickly and can remain in location, and large numbers of pupils or campers can try their compass skills under the direct guidance of their teacher or leader. (Devised by Elston F. Larson.)

GROUP PROJECT—Before the start of this compass competition, each participant needs to know the length of his step. So mark off a distance of 200 feet on the ground over which the participants can walk to determine the length of their steps (as described on pages 53–54).

The compass course for the competition consists of twenty markers placed five feet apart on a straight magnetic east-west line. Number the markers consecutively from 1 to 20, with number 1 on the most westerly marker. An alternate, and simpler, method is to tie two loops in the ends of a piece of binder twine or other strong cord, 100 feet apart, and tie tags numbered from 1 to 20 to this cord, five feet apart. All you have to do, then, is to stretch out the cord between two pegs in an east-west direction, with number 1 on the west end.

When ready to start, each participant is provided with an Orienteering compass and with an instruction card telling him at what mark to start and how to proceed. You will find instructions below for the cards of ten players. If your group is larger, either run the participants in several sections or purchase printed instruction-score

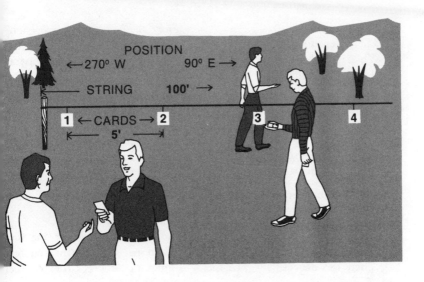

POSITION
← 270° W   90° E →
— STRING   100' →
1 ← CARDS → 2   3   4
|← 5' →|

t takes only a string 100 feet long, plus extra for tying, marked with tags at 5-foot intervals, to set up a Compass Competition for school grounds or camp site.

cards for twenty players from Orienteering Services (see addresses on page 210), or from your local council service center of the Boy Scouts of America.

Start at Point 1
Go   36 degrees for 122 feet
Then 149 degrees for   58 feet
Then 235 degrees for   86 feet

Destination reached: No . . . . .

Start at Point 3
Go   38 degrees for 125 feet
Then 237 degrees for   90 feet
Then 186 degrees for   50 feet

Destination reached: No. . . . .

Start at Point 2
Go   17 degrees for 104 feet
Then 150 degrees for   52 feet
Then 142 degrees for   64 feet

Destination reached: No. . . . .

Start at Point 4
Go   36 degrees for 122 feet
Then 174 degrees for   50 feet
Then 228 degrees for   74 feet

Destination reached: No. . . . .

Start at Point 5
Go   22 degrees for 107 feet
Then 158 degrees for   54 feet
Then 186 degrees for   50 feet

Destination reached: No. ....

Start at Point 6
Go   3 degrees for 100 feet
Then 132 degrees for   74 feet
Then 225 degrees for   69 feet

Destination reached: No. ....

Start at Point 7
Go   34 degrees for 119 feet
Then 186 degrees for   50 feet
Then 228 degrees for   74 feet

Destination reached: No. ....

Start at Point 8
Go   346 degrees for 102 feet
Then 129 degrees for   78 feet
Then 211 degrees for   58 feet

Destination reached: No. ....

Start at Point 9
Go   346 degrees for 102 feet
Then 129 degrees for   78 feet
Then 186 degrees for   50 feet

Destination reached: No. ....

Start at Point 10
Go   343 degrees for 104 feet
Then 141 degrees for   64 feet
Then 145 degrees for   61 feet

Destination reached: No. ....

Each participant goes to the marker which has the number that corresponds to the starting point on his card and proceeds according to instructions. When he has finished, he writes down the number of the marker nearest to the destination he has reached (all the routes lead back to markers on the course line) and turns his card over to the judge. The correct destinations for each of the starting points are found on page 204.

If the player reaches the correct destination he receives a score of 100 points. Otherwise, the judge deducts from his score of 100 points 1 point for each foot of error, or 5 points for each marker from the correct one.

Run the game three times with different starting points for a possible maximum score of 300 points.

COMPASS WALK   OUTDOOR PRACTICE

PURPOSE—Practice in following a cross-country bearing with precision.

For the Compass Walk put up your own markers along the edge of a road or pick a road lined with fence posts at evenly spaced intervals.

GROUP PROJECT—After some practice using the compass, plan a bee-line compass walk over a distance of approximately one-half mile. To lay out the course, locate a stretch of straight road lined with fence posts, or put up your own posts. Tack markers numbered 1 to 10 on ten of these posts, about 100 feet apart. At one of these markers—No. 4, for instance—face at right angle to the line of posts, take the bearing of the direction in which you are faced, and proceed in that direction as carefully as possible for one-half mile, or about 15 minutes.

Place a marker here. This is the starting point for the players. Then add 180° to your bearing if it is below 180°, or subtract 180° from it if it is above 180°. This is your back bearing—the direction from the point where you now are to the post from which you set out—

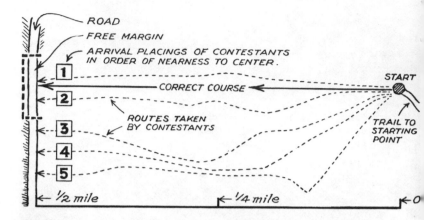

To lay out a Compass Walk course, set out from the Free Margin and hike ½ mile to mark the starting point. Contestants begin at Start and must hit inside the Free Margin.

and the bearing the participants are to follow to reach the correct spot.

Each player is provided with an Orienteering compass and is given the bearing to follow. On a one-half-mile course a margin of 100 feet must be allowed for unavoidable errors. This means that any participant hitting the road between posts marked 3 and 5—if your original post was No. 4—scores a possible 100 points.

A Beeline Out-and-Back Compass Walk

After you have mastered the use of the compass with a fair degree of accuracy over short distances, you are ready for a cross-country compass walk—or "beeline" walk if you prefer.

Take yourself out to some fairly familiar terrain—your local city park, your camp, or some countryside you know. Decide on the compass degree direction in which you want to go. Figure on about half an hour's travel out (that would be approximately one mile) and the same length of time and distance coming back.

When you have arrived at your starting point, set the compass for the number of degrees you have decided on. Then determine the first lap of your journey in the way that should be familiar to you by now:

Hold the compass level before you, with the direction-of-travel arrow pointing straight ahead.

Turn your whole body until the compass needle lies directly over the orienting arrow inside the compass housing, north end toward N.

Look up and decide on a landmark in the direction in which you are sighting.

Proceed directly to the landmark without looking at the compass.

When you have reached the landmark and thus completed the first lap of your beeline walk, sight toward the next landmark in the direction in which you are traveling.

Eventually you will have traveled the distance and the length of time—half an hour—that you had decided on and you are ready for the return journey.

Turn about and do a back-traveling job as described on page 78: Hold the compass level in your hand in the usual manner, but with the direction-of-travel arrow pointing *toward you* instead of away from you. Turn your whole body until your compass is oriented with the north end of the needle pointing at N, raise your eyes, and pick the first landmark for your return trip. And so on.

In another half an hour of back-traveling you are right back at your starting point—or close enough to it to recognize the familiar surroundings.

Overcoming Obstacles

On a cross-country walk there will probably be occasions when there is an obstacle in your way—a lake, a swamp, a building, or any one of a number of things. Well, if you can't walk through or over the obstacle, you'll have to walk around it.

If you CAN see across or through your obstacle it's a comparatively simple matter: locate a prominent landmark on the other side of the obstacle, such as a large tree or a building. Walk to it around the obstacle and take your next bearing from there.

Before setting out again, make certain you are on the right track by taking a *"back-reading"*—looking back toward the point from which you came. That point should be directly behind you—half a circle behind you. You could reset your compass for a back-reading by add-

If you run up against an obstacle which you can see across, pick a prominent landmark on the opposite side of the obstacle and proceed to it.

ing 180 degrees to the compass setting if below 180 degrees, or by subtracting 180 degrees if the setting is above 180 degrees. But rather than complicating matters for yourself with adding or subtracting and later resetting to the original degree number, make use of the direction-of-travel arrow on the base plate of your Orienteering compass:

Don't change the setting of the compass at all. Simply hold the Orienteering compass backwards—with the direction-of-travel arrow pointing *toward* you instead of away from you. Orient the compass in the usual way with the north part of the needle at N. Then sight *against* the direction-of-travel arrow instead of with it and raise your eyes—you should then be looking directly back toward the point from which you came.

If you CAN'T see across or through the obstacle you can walk around it by right angles: turn at a right angle from your route and, counting your steps, walk until you are certain you are beyond the extension of the obstacle in that direction. Then turn at a right angle back on your

After having walked around your obstacle, take a "back-reading" toward the point from which you started to make certain of your course.

original bearing and proceed until you are clear of the obstacle. Again, turn at a right angle back toward your original sighting line and step off the identical number of steps you took during your first direction change. You are now back on your original sighting line. Make another right-angle turn and proceed in your original direction.

You can, of course, make these right-angle turns by resetting the compass at each turn, adding 90 degrees for each turn to the right, or subtracting 90 degrees for each turn to the left from the original compass setting. But why do it the hard way when you can do it without any resetting whatever? You can do it by simply taking advantage of the right angles of the Orienteering compass' base plate:

Let us say that you want to go *to the right around the obstacle* ahead.

For your first right-angle turn, hold your Orienteering compass with the base plate *crosswise* in your hand, with the direction-of-travel arrow pointing toward your *left*, and orient the compass in the usual manner. Sight along the back edge of the base plate, from left

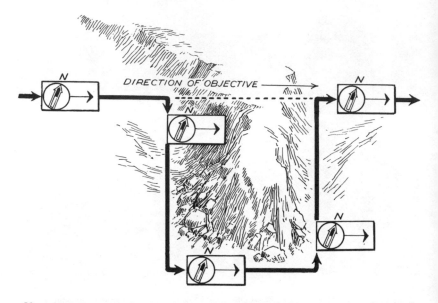

If you can't see across the obstacle walk around it at right angles using the back edge of the Orienteering compass's base plate for sighting.

corner to right corner toward a suitable landmark, and walk enough steps (count them!) toward the landmark to be certain that you are beyond the obstacle in its stretch in that direction.

For the second turn (to the left), hold the compass the usual way, with the direction-of-travel arrow pointing straight ahead of you —you are back on the original bearing—and walk far enough to get well beyond your obstacle in this direction.

For the third turn (again to the left), hold the compass with the base plate *crosswise* again, but with the direction-of-travel arrow to your *right*. You orient the compass and sight along the back edge of the base plate—this time from right corner to left corner—and walk in the new direction exactly the same number of steps you took in your first direction change.

For your final turn (to the right), orient the compass with the direction-of-travel arrow pointing directly ahead of you. The obstacle has been overcome—and you continue toward your destination.

If instead of going to the right of the obstacle it is more convenient for you to *go to the left around the obstacle*, reverse these instructions and hold the base plate in the first turning with the direction-of-travel arrow pointing to the right, in the third turning pointing to the left.

Special Compass Uses for Fishermen and Hunters

For the sake of exploring, traveling by compass is in itself an exciting experience. But if you are a fisherman or a hunter you can put your Orienteering compass to a number of other uses.

Finding a Choice Fishing Lake

Let's say that you are a fisherman always on the look-out for the best possible trout stream or lake.

You've heard of a wonderful fishing lake south-west of the Blackton railway station. It's easy to get there and back with an Orienteering compass.

You have been hearing about Silver Lake from some other fisher-man and want to wet a line there yourself. Silver Lake, your friends tell you, is located directly south-west of the Blackton railway station. But as to getting there—there just isn't any road from Blackton to Silver Lake. You'll have to find your way cross-country.

One beautiful morning, you arrive at Blackton station. From here on it's simple with an Orienteering compass.

You know you have to travel south-west. That would be 225°. So you set your compass for 225° by lining up the 225° mark of the compass housing over the black index pointer of the rim. Compass in hand, direction-of-travel arrow pointing straight ahead, you orient the compass and sight. In that direction lies Silver Lake.

You reach it without difficulty—and Silver Lake proves to live up to its reputation. You get the catch of the year!

When you have reached your limit, you are ready to return to the Blackton station. That's easy, too. You simply backtrack by compass, as described on page 78, by sighting over the compass, but with the base plate's direction-of-travel arrow pointing toward you instead of away from you.

Relocating a Top Fishing Spot

You have been well satisfied with your success along the shores of Silver Lake. But the big ones, they tell you, are way out. So one day you get a boat and try your luck. You throw out a cast or two or three—and then it happens: you nab a really big one! You anchor the boat—that first big fish may be just a stroke of luck—and you cast a few times more. Another one, then another. There is no doubt about the kind of spot it is now. In a short while, you have your limit.

Obviously, that's a place worth remembering, worth coming back to some other day. But it is out in the middle of a large lake and would be difficult to find again.

Or would it? Not with an Orienteering compass. It is simply a mat-ter of taking "cross-bearings," writing down what you find, and using your notes the next time you come around.

To take cross-bearings, pick out two prominent and permanent landmarks on land and determine the directions to them. What will

When you've found an especially good fishing spot in a lake make notes of cross-bearings to two landmarks; use them to find same spot next time.

they be? The large white house may be prominent, but is it permanent? Possibly not—it may be painted red by the time you come back again. The big tree? It might be cut down. The large cliff at the shore? Excellent. The boat dock where you rented the boat? Of course. If no boat dock, you will have to decide on another permanent landmark.

To find the bearing to the cliff point the direction-of-travel arrow toward the cliff and turn the compass housing until the compass is oriented—until the north part of the needle points to N. Read the number of degrees on the edge of the compass housing at the base of the direction line. What is it? 113°.

Next, point the direction-of-travel arrow toward the boat dock and again orient the compass. What is the reading to the dock? 32°.

Write down in your notebook: "Excellent fishing spot, Silver Lake, 113° to cliff, 32° to boat dock."

The next time you decide to go fishing, rent your boat, get out your notes, and set out:

The direction from the fishing spot to the boat dock was 32°. Obviously, then, the direction from the boat dock to the fishing spot is half a circle the other way. You therefore add 180° to the 32°, making it 212°. (If the original figure had been larger than 180°, you would subtract 180° instead of add.) Set your compass by turning the compass housing until the 212° mark is located directly over the black index pointer of the rim. Point the direction-of-travel arrow straight over the bow of your boat and have your rowing friend turn the boat until the north part of the compass needle points to N. Raise your head and locate a landmark on the opposite shore—let's say a rock—and have your friend row directly toward it.

Now reset the compass to 113°—the reading toward the cliff. Orient the compass in your hand, north part of the needle on N, and continue sighting over the direction-of-travel arrow while your friend goes on with his rowing.

You are almost there—the arrow almost hits the cliff. A little farther. Out goes your anchor. And in goes your line. Up come the fish—we hope.

Hunting in a General Direction

Instead of fishing, hunting may be your bent. Here also the Orienteering compass comes in handy.

Let's say that you want to hunt in a north-westerly direction from your hunting camp. There were plenty of deer that way last year, as you well remember!

Set the compass at north-west—that would be 315°—by turning the compass housing until the 315° mark is over the black index pointer of the rim. Hold the compass with the direction-of-travel arrow pointing straight ahead and orient the compass with the north part of the needle toward N. The arrow points the way you want to go. As you walk, check with your compass occasionally to be sure you are holding to the general direction on which you had decided.

When you feel you've had enough hunting for the day and want to return to camp, check your direction again. But this time hold the compass—*without changing its setting*—with the direction-of-travel ar-

You got your deer—now to get help bringing it out. Follow your Orienteering compass to the nearest road, later backtrack with the same compass setting.

row pointing toward you instead of ahead of you and backtrack as explained on page 78.

"Pinpointing" Your Prize Kill

Some day you may be in real luck: you get that big ten-point buck you have been dreaming about. Your thrill remains after you have dressed-out the heavy animal. But how to get it back to camp—that's the problem. It is much too heavy for you to handle alone. You need help. But finding the critter later would be like hunting for a needle in a haystack—if it weren't for your Orienteering compass.

You plan your strategy: you know from your general knowledge of the lay of the land that there's a road half a mile or so south-east of you and that it leads to the hunting lodge where it should be easy to get assistance.

So you mark the location of your buck with something easily seen from a distance—a white handkerchief tied to a nearby tree, for instance. Then set your compass for south-east (135°) and start off, following accurately the direction toward which the direction-of-travel arrow points. Pick out landmarks on the line of travel and proceed from landmark to landmark. Count your double-steps carefully as you go to be sure of your distance.

You reach the road—it took you 512 double-steps. Mark the spot clearly with some dead limbs, a log, or a pile of rocks, which you can recognize later, then proceed to the lodge.

You line up your helpers (and possibly a pack horse or a jeep or some other conveyance if one is available) and travel back up the road until you reach the spot marked.

Now it's a matter of backtracking. Your compass is already set—you haven't disturbed the setting at all. All you have to do is to follow the compass in the opposite direction from before by sighting against the direction-of-travel arrow instead of with it, sighting landmark after landmark in that direction, and counting off your double-steps—512. Where is the deer? Well, you can't expect to hit it right on the nose even if it were a champion-size deer. But it should be close by. Mark the point you have reached, then circle it in an ever-widening spiral. There's the white handkerchief on the tree. And there's the deer!

PART III

Fun with Map and Compass Together

Now that you know the functions of map and compass separately you will want to use them together for finding your way and for getting your first taste of the thrilling sport of Orienteering—the up-to-date name for the art of traveling through unknown territory with map and compass and the very best way of practicing navigation in the woods.

There's real enjoyment of the out-of-doors ahead of you. You will increase the fun of your outings as your trips take you cross-country, off the beaten track, away from the old familiar paths. There are new things to see, new things to experience. And there is excitement, too—the excitement of the uncertain: "Am I on the right trail? . . .

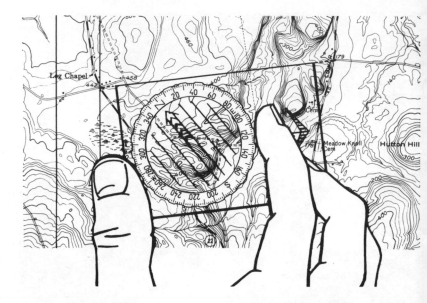

FIRST STEP in setting your compass by the map: place the base plate on the map in such a way that one edge of it connects start with destination.

Will I hit the tip of the lake? . . . Can I get through or must I pick another route? . . . Is that my goal right ahead of me now? . . ."

In the beginning you may want to do some Orienteering on your own, but your greatest Orienteering thrills will come when you join forces with other orienteers.

Your First Orienteering Trip—At Home

Before you set out on an actual Orienteering trip in the field, let's see what is involved by taking the trip first at home on the training map in the back of the book. So open the map and lay a route on it.

Let's say that you want to start your trip at the crossroads ¼ inch southeast of the letter "l" in Log Chapel—or, according to our map-reading "shorthand": ¼" SE l in Log Chapel. A short, suitable expedition might then take in the road-T north of Meadow Knoll Ceme-

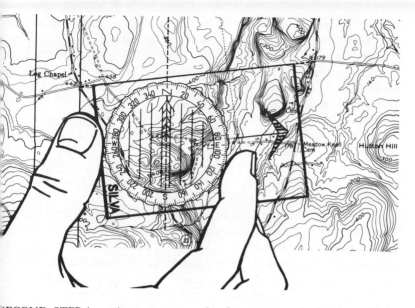

ery, the farmhouse west of Niger Marsh, the crossroads north of the Log Chapel, and back to your starting point—see map on page 108.

Setting Your Compass

Your first job is to set your Orienteering compass for the first lap of the journey—from the crossroads south-east of Log Chapel to the road-T 1⅜ inches north-west of the **H** in Hutton Hill.

You have probably already bought yourself an Orienteering compass. This is where it gets a workout. On the other hand, if you haven't gotten around to buying one yet, you can get along at this stage of the game with the training compass in the envelope in the back of the book. The reason you can manage with the needleless training compass is that the compass needle plays no part in the planning of an Orienteering trip—you only make use of the compass hous-

ing with its degree markings and the base plate together as a protractor, transferring the direction from map to compass.

Place the compass on the training map with one side of the base
plate connecting the starting point at the crossroads with your first
destination at the road-T and with the direction-of-travel arrow
pointing in the direction you intend to go.

Then twist the compass housing until the orienting arrow on the inside of the housing lies parallel to the nearest north line—meridian—
of the map, with the north point up.

Your Orienteering compass is now set for the first lap. What is the
setting? Check the degree number at the point of the compass housing
touched by the direction line. 84°? Correct!

By orienting the actual compass in the field, then following the
direction-of-travel arrow, you should have no difficulty hitting your
first destination.

Next lap: from road-T to the farmhouse ¾ inches west of **N** in
Niger Marsh. Again, place the compass on the map with the side edge
of the base plate connecting the two points and twist the compass
housing until the orienting arrow lies parallel with a map north line,
with north to the top. Your compass is set for your next lap. How
many degrees?

Next set the compass from the farmhouse west of Niger Marsh to
the crossroads 1⅛ inches north of the **l** in Log Chapel, and finally for
the lap from the crossroads back to the point from which you started.

Your Distances

You now have the compass settings you will use on the way, but
there is something else in which you should be interested: the dis
tances.

Go over the route again to find the "air-line" distances between the
different points. For this, use the inch rule along the side edge of the
base plate of your compass. The map is in the scale of 1:24,000. Each
inch, therefore, is 2,000 feet. In measuring, you should arrive at these
results:

Crossroads to road-T N Meadow Knoll Cemetery	7,100 feet
Road-T to farm W Niger Marsh	2,700 feet
Farm to crossroads N Log Chapel	7,300 feet
Crossroads to starting point	2,700 feet
Total distance	19,800 feet

A distance of about 3¾ miles which you shouldn't have too much trouble covering in around two hours—unless you run into unexpected obstacles.

Indoor Map-and-Compass Practices—Use training compass and training map until setting your compass by map becomes second nature to you.

COMPASS SETTING QUIZ   INDOOR PRACTICE

PURPOSE—To become familiar with setting the Orienteering compass for different directions on the map.

TEST YOURSELF—Open up the training map and bring out the training compass. Locate the crossroads ¼ inch south-east of the letter **l** in Log Chapel. That is your starting point. Now determine the degree bearings to the following points:

1. Starting point to Post 1, at church ⅜ inch north-north-west of **M** in Meadow Knoll Cemetery . . . .°

2. From Post 1 to Post 2, located at road-T ¹¹/₁₆ inch W **N** in Niger Marsh . . . .°

3. From Post 2 to Post 3, at farmhouse 1½ inches NW **H** in Huckleberry Mtn . . . .°

4. From Post 3 to Post 4, barn ⅜ inch NW **B** in Charter Brook . . . .°

5. From Post 4 to Goal, at road-T ¼ inch N **k** in Sucker Brook . . . .°

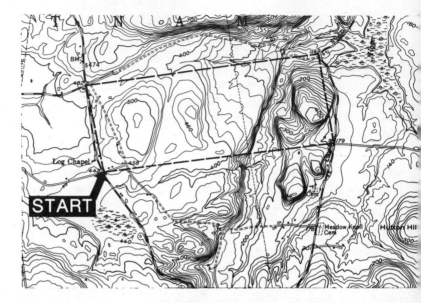

Open up the training map in the back of the book and locate the territory of the route shown above, of the trip described on pages 104–5.

(Check your readings against the correct answers on page 204.)

AS GAME—Each player is provided with a copy of the training map, training compass (see Orienteering Training Kit, page 210), pencil, and a copy of this listing. On signal, the players determine the bearings. The player finishing in the shortest time with the most correct answers wins.

WHAT DO YOU FIND?   INDOOR PRACTICE

PURPOSE—Practice in making correct measurements and determining compass bearings on the map.

TEST YOURSELF—Using training map and training compass, determine the landscape features located at these points:

1. Distance: 2,400 feet.
   Direction: 298° from **H** in **H**utton Hill . . . .

2. Distance: 4,000 feet.
   Direction: 182° from **R** in **R**ecord Hill . . . .

3. Distance: 1,000 feet.
   Direction: 68° from **s** in Anthony**s** Nose . . . .

4. Distance: 2,100 feet.
   Direction: 174° from **U** in **PU**TNAM . . . .

5. Distance: 2,200 feet.
   Direction: 24° from **r** in Sucke**r** Brook . . . .

(The answers are found on page 204.)

AS GAME—Each player has a training map, training compass, paper and pencil, and a copy of the listing given above. Players have ten minutes in which to finish the task. Correct answers score 20 points. The player with the largest score wins.

Compass Declination (or Variation)

For your first actual Orienteering trip let's take for granted that the training map is the actual map of the territory in which you do your Orienteering and that the route you have just planned is the one you want to follow.

You arrive at your starting point at the crossroads south of Log Chapel. Open up your map, line up the side edge of the base plate of the compass to connect the starting point with the road-T north of Meadow Knoll Cemetery, and twist the compass housing to line up the orienting arrow with a north line on the map. Hold the compass with the direction-of-travel arrow pointing straight ahead of you, the north part of the compass needle pointing to the N of the compass housing, and line up a landmark in front of you. Now you are set to be on your way.

Or are you?

You would be if the *true north* of your map were the same as the

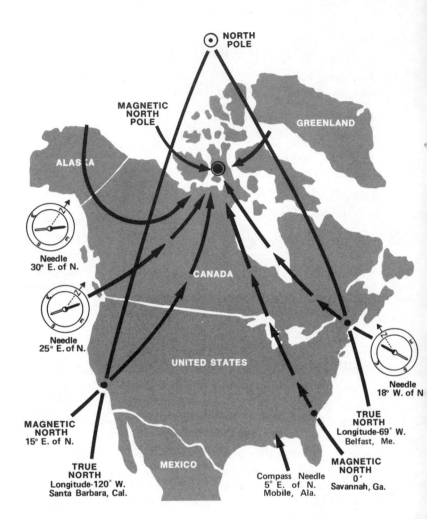

True north is the map direction toward the geographical North Pole; magnetic north is the compass direction toward the Magnetic North Pole.

magnetic north of your compass and the geology of our continent didn't affect the magnetized needle. But unfortunately, they aren't and it does.

The result is that true north and magnetic north are the same only along a line that runs off the east coast of Florida, through Lake Michigan, and on up to the Magnetic North Pole located north of Hudson Bay. On any location between this zero line and the Atlantic the compass needle points west of the true-north line. On any location between the zero line and the Pacific the compass needle points east of

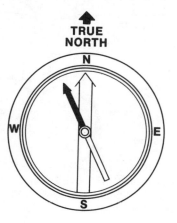

The magnetic force of the earth pulls the compass needle out of line with the true-north direction. The angle between the two directions is the "declination."

the true-north line. The angle between the direction the compass needle points and the true-north line is called "declination" or "variation." It varies from 20° west (20° W) in Maine, to 30° east (30° E) in parts of Alaska.

Locate your area on the maps on pages 110 and 112 and find the compass declination for your territory. Repeat it to yourself again and again until it is firmly established in your mind.

If you are traveling away from your home territory, check the compass declination in the bottom margin of the map you will be using (see page 34).

What Difference Does the Declination Make?

Why is it so important to know the declination of your location? Because you may be thrown completely off your intended course if

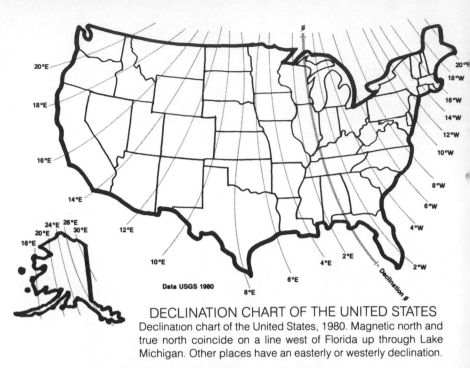

DECLINATION CHART OF THE UNITED STATES
Declination chart of the United States, 1980. Magnetic north and true north coincide on a line west of Florida up through Lake Michigan. Other places have an easterly or westerly declination.

you depend on a compass direction taken from a map without taking the declination into consideration.

Let's assume a location where the declination is 15° W. Set your Orienteering compass and blithely take off in the direction the direction-of-travel arrow points. Your course will be 15° off. Whatever distance you travel, each degree off will result in an error of ¹/₆₀ of the distance traveled. After you have traveled a distance of 3,000 feet, you will be *50 feet off for each degree of declination*—a total, in this particular case where the declination is 15°, of 15 times 50 feet, or 750 feet. If you continue, *you will be one-quarter mile off after one mile of traveling.* No wonder you can't find your destination!

Fortunately, it is a simple matter on a modern Orienteering compass to compensate for declination so that a wrong direction will not throw you off your course. It can be done in one of two ways: by resetting the compass each time you set it from the map *or*, what is much easier, by making your map speak "compass language." (Note: There are also Orienteering compasses with a declination setting device built in.)

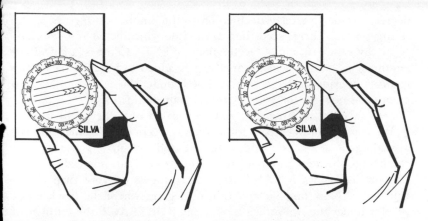

To compensate if declination is WEST: check the number of degrees at the base of the direction line. ADD the declination and reset your compass to the new number.

Resetting Your Compass for Declination

If your declination is WEST: set your compass on your map in the usual way. Now find your setting in degrees where the black index pointer under the rim indicates it to be. ADD the number of

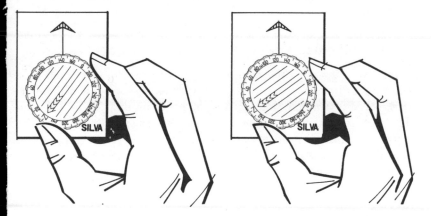

To compensate if declination is EAST: check the number of degrees at the base of the direction line. SUBTRACT declination and reset your compass to the new number.

degrees of your westerly declination to the number of degrees of the setting you read here, according to the rule remembered among orienteers by the rhyme "Declination WEST—Compass BEST"—anything is "better" when something is added to it. Then twist the compass housing so that the index line is under the new number. The compass is now set for your map and your declination.

Let's take an example: let's say you live where the declination is 9° W. You set your compass for a certain direction on the map and get a reading of 282°. You add 9 to 282 and get 291. You reset the compass to this new number (291°) and are ready to proceed.

If your declination is EAST: set your compass on your map in the usual way. Now find your setting in degrees where the black index pointer under the rim indicates it to be. SUBTRACT the number of degrees of your easterly declination from the number of degrees of the setting you read here, according to the rule remembered among orienteers by the rhyme "Declination EAST—Compass LEAST"—with something subtracted, the setting becomes "less" than it was. Then twist the compass housing so that the index pointer is under the new number. The compass is now set for your map and your declination.

Let's take an example: let's say you live where the declination is 18° E. You set your compass for a certain direction on the map and get a reading of 144°. You subtract 18 from 144 and get 126. You reset your compass to this new number (126°) and are ready to proceed.

Making Your Map Speak "Compass Language"

Instead of going to the trouble of resetting the compass each time you take a direction from the map, with the possibility of making errors, there is a much simpler way of compensating for declination. This way consists in providing the map with magnetic-north lines. By using these lines instead of the true-north lines of the regular meridians your map speaks the same language as your compass. The settings you take on your compass using these lines do not require resetting to compensate for declination—the declination is taken care of automatically.

There are two ways of providing your map with these magnetic-north lines.

Using the map's magnetic-north line—The simplest method is to draw a line, with great care, up through the map in continuation of the magnetic-north half-arrow line in the bottom margin of the topographic map (in the right margin of the instruction map in the back of this book). Then draw other lines parallel to this line, 1 or 2 inches apart (see illustration below). NOTE: Take time off from your reading right now to draw such magnetic-north lines on your instruction map.

This method works well in most cases but has a couple of drawbacks:

Since the magnetic line on the diagram is very short any straight-edge extension could result in considerable error. Also, in the cases of very small angles the diagrams are sometimes exaggerated for the sake of clarity. So to be perfectly sure when using this method, first check the diagram angle between the magnetic-north half-arrow line and the true-north line to make certain that this angle is actually the number of degrees indicated.

Using the Orienteering compass—For a more exact method use an Orienteering compass as a protractor.

For a map of an area with *westerly declination*, subtract the number

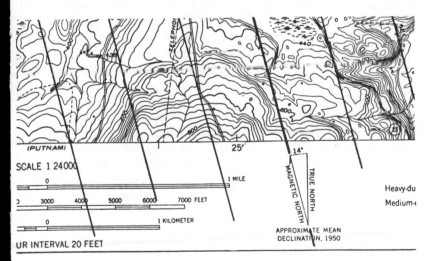

Make your map speak "compass language" by providing it with magnetic-north lines. The method shown here makes use of the map's declination diagram.

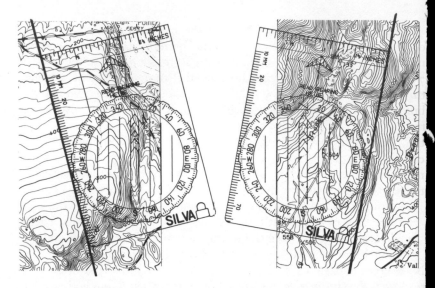

For a more precise way of making your map speak "compass language," set the Orienteering compass for the declination and use the map border as a guide.

of declination degrees from 360° (north) and set the compass dial at
that number. If the declination is 14° W, for instance, you would set
the dial at 346° (360° minus 14°). Now place the compass on the map.
Align the north lines on the bottom of the transparent compass housing with the right border line of the map and draw your first magnetic-north line along the left edge of the base plate, then add other
lines parallel to this.

For a map of an area with *easterly declination*, add the number of declination degrees to 0° (north) and set the compass dial at that number.
If the declination is 10° E, for instance, you would set the dial at 10°.
Place the compass on the map. Align the north lines on the bottom of
the transparent compass housing with the left border line of the map
and draw your first magnetic-north line along the right edge of the
base plate, then add other lines parallel to this.

By using these magnetic-north lines whenever you take a bearing
from the map, you can forget that there ever was such a thing as a
declination problem.

It can happen that the meridians—true-north lines—on your map do not run parallel to the side margins. On your training map there is no problem. The lower right corner indicates the longitude, 73°22′30″, and you find the same in the upper right corner. To check this on a map on which the longitude is not indicated at the corners but on the lower and upper margins, draw a meridian from a longitude number in the lower margin of the map to the same number in the upper margin. If this line is parallel to the side margins, then you can use either the margins or this line for drawing your magnetic-north lines. If this line is off, then you have to draw your magnetic-north lines on the basis of the meridian line.

TRAVELING BY MAP AND COMPASS— ORIENTEERING

Now that you know how to use map and compass together you are ready for honest-to-goodness Orienteering in the field. Start off with a couple of short cross-country hikes through easy territory to practice up on your map-and-compass skills. If you live in a big city, you can do your practicing in one of its larger parks—provided you can secure a detailed map of it.

Later you can plan longer trips through tougher terrain—and, finally, graduate into a full-fledged orienteer, confident of your Orienteering ability and completely at home in true wilderness areas.

Getting Ready for Orienteering in the Field

For your first Orienteering hike get out the topographic map of your local area and plan a course to follow.

Choose an easily accessible starting point, pick four or five points in the terrain which you would be interested in finding, and plan to wind up your trip at the place from which you started. Decide whether you want to take the hike alone or with a friend.

Then, at last, on the day you have set, you arrive at your starting point, rarin' to go.

But before getting under way, orient your map to get a general idea of the lay of the land and the trip that's ahead.

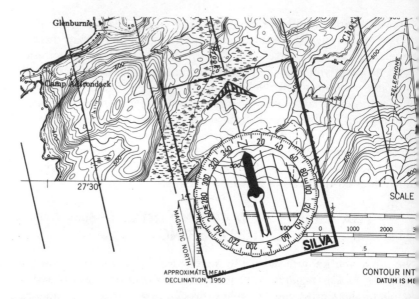

One way of orienting map with compass is to place the edge of the base plate parallel with the magnetic-north line, then turn the map until the compass on it is oriented.

Orienting the Map with a Compass

Orienting a map, as you know from your map work (pages 51–52), means lining up the directions of the map with the same directions in the field. You can do it "by inspection" as already described (page 52), but it is an even simpler matter to orient it "by compass."

There are two ways of doing this:

Using Map's Declination Diagram—Set the Orienteering compass at 360°. Then place it on the map so that the side edge of the base plate lies parallel with the magnetic-north line of the declination diagram in the margin of your map and with the direction-of-travel arrow toward north. Then turn the map with the compass lying on it until the north part of the compass needle points to the N of the compass housing. The compass is now oriented—and so is the map.

Using Map's Magnetic-North Lines—Set the Orienteering compass at 360°. Then place it on the map so that the side edge of the base plate lies along one of the magnetic-north lines you have drawn on the map (as described on page 115) and with the direction-of-travel arrow toward north. Then turn the map with the compass lying on it until the north part of the compass needle points to the N of the compass housing. The map is now oriented.

Using Map and Compass in Orienteering

While it is advantageous to spread out and orient the map at the start of an Orienteering hike to get a general idea of the lay of the land and of the route you intend to follow, it is really unnecessary, when you use the Orienteering compass, to repeatedly orient it as you travel along the route. To get your bearings for Orienteering, simply open the map to that small part containing the stretch of the route directly ahead of you and transfer the direction you want to follow from the map to your compass. With directions of map and compass now coinciding, it is simple to keep them oriented together as you proceed.

The Three Basic Steps in Traveling by Compass and Map

To travel from point to point in the field, follow the three simple steps: place your compass on the map, set your compass by the map, and set yourself by the compass (see illustrations pages 120–21)

STEP 1. *On the Map, Line Up Your Compass with Your Route.*
Place the Orienteering compass on the map with edge of its base plate touching both your starting point and your destination, with the base plate's direction-of-travel arrow pointing in the direction you want to go. Disregard the compass needle.

STEP 2. *On the Compass, Set Housing to Direction of Your Route.*
Hold the base plate firmly against the map with your left hand. With your right hand, turn the compass housing until the orienting arrow on the bottom of the housing lies parallel to the nearest magnetic-north line drawn on your map, with arrow-point to the top. Disregard the compass needle. The compass is now set for the direction

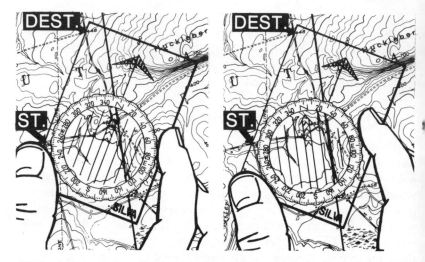

STEP 1 in Orienteering—On the map, line up the compass with the route from Start (ST.) to Destination (DEST.).
STEP 2 in Orienteering—On the compass, set the housing by aligning the orienting arrow with the magnetic-north line.

of your destination. By using the drawn-in magnetic-north line you have automatically compensated for any compass declination in the area covered by your map.

STEP 3. *In the Field, Follow the Direction Set on the Compass.*

Hold the compass level in front of you with the direction-of-travel arrow pointing straight ahead. Turn yourself by shifting your feet while watching the compass needle until the needle lies directly over the orienting arrow on the bottom of the compass housing, with the North end of the needle pointing to N. The direction-of-travel arrow now points to your destination. Raise your head, choose a landmark—a rock or a large tree or some other sighting point—in that direction. Walk to that landmark without looking at your compass or your map. When you have reached it, again check the direction with your compass on which you have been careful not to change the setting. Ahead is another landmark leading to your destination.

STEP 3 in Orienteering—In the field, follow the direction set on the compass. Hold the compass level in your hand. Turn yourself until the needle points to N on the housing. The direction-of-travel arrow now gives the direction to your destination.

With compass oriented, raise your eyes and pick a landmark in the direction in which the direction-of-travel arrow points. Walk to this landmark, then sight with the compass to the next landmark along your route. Continue to your destination.

When you have reached the first point of your Orienteering hike, study your map again and set the compass for the next lap of your journey.

And so on until you have covered the whole route and are back at your starting point with a feeling of accomplishment, your first Orienteering expedition a success.

Try an Imaginary Orienteering "Hike"

After you have done some short-distance Orienteering on your own or with a couple of friends, you'll surely want to try your newly acquired Orienteering skills on a more ambitious scale. Then it becomes a matter of planning a map course through unfamiliar territory of about five miles or more—depending on how energetic you are—and then traveling over the course in the field with map and compass.

To give you an idea of what you may experience on such an Orienteering hike, open up the training map in the back of the book, decide on a number of points you want to hit, and try to figure out how you would proceed from point to point if you were actually out in that area. As an example, let's say that you've picked the points indicated on the maps on pages 124 and 125—starting at the road-T north of Meadow Knoll Cemetery and winding up in the same spot after a clockwise trip.

Clothing and Equipment

Now, if this were a real hike, you would need to consider your clothing and necessary equipment before setting out.

For comfort on an Orienteering hike you'll want to dress in old, familiar clothes suitable for the season of the year. Pay special attention to your socks—no binding or chafing here; and to your shoes—no sneakers or soft-soled moccasins for this kind of activity.

For equipment you'll need a topographic map of the territory, your Orienteering compass, a watch, and a pencil.

You'll probably want to bring along a pocket lunch and a couple of candy bars for sustenance and quick energy, and possibly, during the summer, a canteen of water.

Your Outdoor Manners

Make up your mind in all your Orienteering to live up to the best traditions and manners of the true outdoorsman. In this respect, you can do nothing better than to follow the Outdoor Code developed by the Boy Scouts of America as part of a national good turn:

"As an American, I will do my best to:
"Be clean in my outdoor habits. I will treat the outdoors as a heritage to be improved for our greater enjoyment. I will keep my trash and garbage out of America's waters, fields, woods and roadways.
"Be careful with fire. I will prevent wild fire. I will build my fire in a safe place, and be sure it is dead out before I leave.
"Be considerate in the outdoors. I will treat public and private property with respect. I will remember that use of the outdoors is a privilege I can lose by abuse.
"Be conservation-minded. I will learn how to practice good conservation of soil, waters, forests, minerals, grasslands, and wildlife; and I will urge others to do the same. I will use sportsmanlike methods in all my outdoor activities."

The Outdoor Code is clear in itself. A few of its points apply especially to the orienteer:
In traveling cross-country you will probably at times encounter areas where fire hazards exist, caused by summer drought, down timber, dry leaves or grass or weed-stalks. A spark may set off a conflagration. For this reason it is a self-imposed rule among orienteers never to smoke en route. Many of them go a step further and refrain from even carrying cigarettes on their persons while Orienteering.
Consideration of property is of prime importance in Orienteering. Never trespass private property—permission usually will be cheerfully given. When crossing the property, with permission, don't walk over planted fields; leave gates the way you found them; leave farm animals undisturbed. When it comes to public property, heed the advice of "the man with the badge"—the park ranger, forest ranger, or game warden. Follow the regulations for the use of the area.

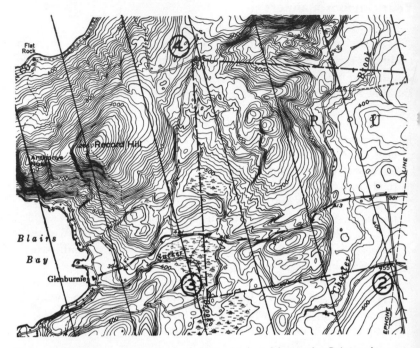

Open up the training map in the back of the book and locate the Orienteering route shown on these two pages. You start at S (Start), . . .

Be Systematical—Steps in Orienteering

Properly clothed and equipped and with the best resolutions in the world in regard to your outdoor manners, you arrive at the spot you have designated as your starting point. You are eager to be on the way.

Not so fast.

For successful Orienteering there are certain practices which expert orienteers have found of value. Better get into the habit of following them from the beginning.

So instead of rushing off on your imaginary hike, take your time and go about things systematically:

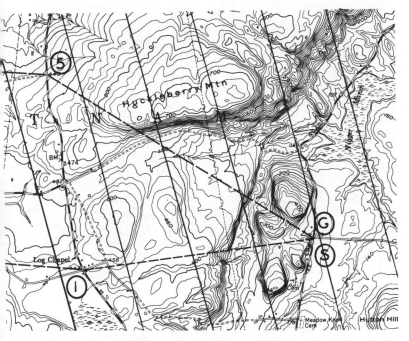

. . proceed in a clockwise direction, and wind up at G (Goal). A description of what you will encounter en route is found on pages 127–28.

1. *Find your exact location on your map.*
That's easy for the starting point. You are right there at the road-T north of Meadow Knoll Cemetery.

2. *Find the exact location on your map of the point to which you are to go and check the general direction to it.*
Study the map. The first point you want to hit is located at the crossroads a few hundred feet south-east of the Log Chapel—or, using map designation: ¼ inch SE of the I in Log Chapel. There it is, approximately 7,000 feet to the west of your starting point.

3. *Draw in the beeline from the place where you are to the point to which you want to go.*

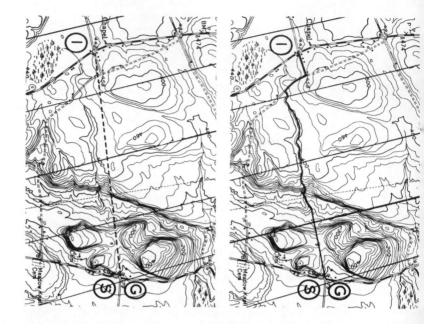

The first lap of your imaginary Orienteering hike. Instead of taking a beeline, follow the brook, then roads, to the first destination.

Get out your pencil, then use the edge of the base plate of your compass to draw in this beeline.

4. Decide on the most efficient route.
Take a good look at your map. The beeline from your starting point to your first destination goes through a level stretch then continues downhill, across a brook, up a cliff, then over level ground. There are no specific landmarks on that line to help you determine whether you are on the right track or not. But by changing your course slightly you will have plenty of help: you can cross a brook and follow a tributary almost the whole way to your destination (see maps). And that is what you do.

5. Set the compass correctly for cross-country traveling.
Set the compass on the map from your starting point to the spot

where the tributary runs into the brook. What is the setting? 270°—correct!

6. *Jot down the time you set out from one point to the next.*
Your map gives you the distance between the two points, and knowing the distance you can figure out the approximate time it'll take you to get to the next point. When that time is up you should be close to your goal and by watching your surroundings you should have no trouble locating it.

Off You Go!

Now, at last, you are set. You proceed on the route you have decided on from your starting point to point 1 of your Orienteering course.

The first stretch is up over a cow pasture, with steep hills on either side of you. You reach the crest of the pasture and run downhill now, through a grove of white cedars. At the bottom of the slope you find the brook meandering along in slow motion.

You didn't hit the brook-T where the tributary comes in, but it should be nearby. Upstream or downstream? Study the map. The brook you intend to follow falls down over the cliff that is in front of you—you should be able to hear it. You listen. There it is—a bit upstream to your left. You climb the cliff right next to the gurgling water. It is a steep climb, but you make it. And then it is easy—the rest is level ground.

You reach the dirt road where it bridges the brook, jog northwestward of the road-T, then west until you reach the crossroads south of Log Chapel. All along, check your route on the training map.

You have reached your first destination according to plan. You are proud! You feel good! That first lap was really something. There's a bit of excitement in your blood now and you're eager to be off to the next point—the crossroads ¾ inch on the map east of the **e** in the Charter Brook, about 2,800 feet in a west-north-westerly direction from where you are now.

You find the location on the map and lay out the beeline. There's nothing to this one. The beeline almost follows a road directly to your second point. Just to be sure, you check the direction of the road with the compass and then you are on the way. You reach the point in short order and prepare to proceed to point number 3—the road-bend $^1/_{16}$ inch north of the **B** in Sucker **B**rook. You have a pretty long stretch before you—5,800 feet toward WSW.

For Speed: Use Roads

You draw the beeline on the map. It crosses the Charter Brook, then strikes some steep slopes and skirts the tip of a swamp. Instead of following the straight line you figure it will be easier and faster to take the road south-westward to the farmhouse. Cross the Charter Brook here (the farmer probably has a footbridge over the brook which he will let you use) and continue between two low hills and along the north edge of the swamp.

And that's exactly what you do. Follow the road to the first farmhouse on the right, get the farmer's permission to cross his land and use the bridge. Then take a new bearing toward the road, leading between the two low hills, then just north of the swamp and to the road. In order to avoid the swamp you had to take the bearing to the road north of the road bend you are looking for, so when you come to the road you turn south on it and you find the spot. Here you study what to do about reaching point number 4, for which you have picked the road-Y 1½ inches NNE of the **l** in Record Hill—about 7,200 feet N of the spot where you are. The beeline to point 4 would be pretty tough: through a swamp, uphill, downhill, another swamp, then steeply uphill along a stream. So, very smartly, you choose the roads instead—north until you hit your destination.

Then to point number 5—the road-T ⅝ inch NNE of the **T** in PUTNAM, about 7,900 feet to the east.

Cross-Country Next

This may be a real toughie—a mile and a half of cross-country going. Study the beeline you have drawn. Maybe not so tough after all—not if you strike out for the brook, follow this to the farmhouse, then proceed south on the road until you hit the footpath, then east on the footpath and the unimproved road.

Set your compass for the farmhouse and start off. It's level ground at first but then it goes downhill, with hemlock-covered slopes on both sides of you. Among a heap of boulders you find the bubbling spring that is the source of the brook. You make your way along the stream through a carpet of ferns, then along grassy banks until you hit the farmhouse. Take a look out over the valley—this would be a spot to come back to: there's a beaver hut right down there in Charter Brook. You enjoy the view but soon decide to continue on your route, southward along the road then eastward along the path.

But where is that path? It should be right there at the road bend. Not a sign of it! Fortunately, you are prepared for such a situation by having counted your steps from the farm. The location is right—it's just that the path has been filled with a maze of undergrowth. You will have to go by compass and hope to strike the unimproved road that leads to point number 5.

Set your compass and continue. And sure enough, this is the path, for there is a footbridge across Charter Brook and a log across a tiny tributary.

And there is the unimproved road and ahead of you the road-T you are aiming for.

One more stretch to go now—back to your starting point at the road-T 1¼ inches north of the **a** in Me**a**dow Knoll Cemetery. How far? About 9,500 feet SE.

There's Always Another Way

Locate the goal on the map. The beeline looks really rough. It climbs up over part of Huckleberry Mountain, down a steep cliff, continues over level territory, then down another cliff, up a steep hill, and down on the other side. There must be another way, an easier way to get there.

There is.

You decide to cut off a corner of Huckleberry Mountain and hit the unimproved dirt road south of it, then east on the road until you hit the highway, and finally south on the highway to your goal.

You set your compass at 146° and continue your journey.

It is fairly easy going now, over bare rocks in spots, but from time

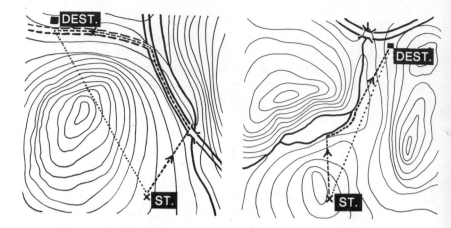

The good orienteer picks the most efficient route. (Left) Instead of climbing a mountain, aim for the bridge and follow the roads. (Right) Strike for a "catching" landmark, such as a lakeshore, to get closer to your destination, then go by compass from there.

to time among down pine, huckleberry bushes, and through brambles. You reach the dirt road—it is only a wagon rut but with a beautiful shady lane with overhanging branches. And you are glad that you decided against climbing Huckleberry Mountain and sliding down its side—you pass a spot where you have a good view of the cliff: a sheer drop of close to three hundred feet!

You're nearly home free now; you don't even have to use your compass on this stretch—the map alone tells you where to go.

And so you finally hit the main road just west of Niger Marsh and continue southward until you reach the road-T at the Meadow Knoll Cemetery.

Now for the Real Thing!

Your first Orienteering "hike" has come to an end. How did you like it? Although traveled in the imagination it sounded like quite an interesting expedition, didn't it? Well, you would have enjoyed the trip a great deal more if you had actually covered the route in the field. So why not decide to set out on a real Orienteering hike at the earliest possible moment? By now you know enough about the use of map and compass to enjoy a fairly ambitious undertaking. So get going!

You will return home well satisfied with yourself. You may have made a few minor mistakes en route—but that's the way to learn. With each Orienteering hike you pick up new pointers—especially if you sit down after you get home and review your excursion by taking a second turn over the route, this time on your map only.

And then there's another Orienteering trip to be planned—and another and another.

In the future the whole outdoors will challenge you to use your skill in finding your way across her widespread acres.

Then Orienteering becomes far more to you than a new skill learned—it becomes your means of being your own guide in locating hidden fishing streams off the beaten track; in undertaking more ambitious hunting expeditions; in vacationing by canoe in some beautiful lake-land wilderness.

For although Orienteering, as such, is interesting and enjoyable, it is not an end in itself—its main purpose is to give you practice, practice, and still more practice in the proper and intelligent use of map and compass for finding your way in unknown territory.

HINTS ON WILDERNESS ORIENTEERING

If you are the ambitious kind of an outdoorsman, you will eventually want to use your Orienteering skills for extensive traveling through wilderness areas.

Such traveling is not for beginners. There are many related skills which must be mastered before you can undertake a sojourn of a week or a month through unfamiliar wilderness territory.

Training for Wilderness Traveling

In addition to the ability to use compass and map correctly in Orienteering, there are other skills that will be required of you if you expect your expedition to be a success:

On a canoe trip the Orienteering compass makes it possible for you to travel in straight lines toward river mouths or portage points.

Hiking Skills—For a short hike near home you need no special equipment and little hike training, but covering an extended route is a different story. You must know what footgear and clothing to use; how to walk most effortlessly; when and how to rest; safety on the trail; trail first aid, in case of a possible accident far away from doctor and hospital.

Backpacking Skills—When your trip calls for spending several nights in the open, you should know how to take care of yourself: what equipment to pick and how to carry it; what food you need, how to transport it, how to prepare it; what camp site to choose, how to pitch a tent and prepare a camp bed; how to build a fire, and how to be positive that it is extinguished after use; what sanitary arrangements are necessary; how to leave a clean camp site.

Canoeing Skills—If you expect to do all or much of your traveling by canoe, a lot of specialized training is necessary before you set out: you need to be a good swimmer, completely at home in the water. And you need to know how to handle a canoe: how to launch and land it; what strokes to use in paddling under various conditions; how to prepare the canoe for portage; the actual technique of portaging; how to be safe on rivers and lakes under all possible weather conditions.

These skills can be mastered only in the field. If you are or have been a member of an outdoor club or one of our major youth movements—the Boy Scouts or the Girl Scouts—you will probably already have had your share of hiking and camping, swimming and canoeing. Otherwise, you will have to get your training by tying in with some local group of outdoorsmen.

Certain books may be of assistance to you by suggesting methods and shortcuts. General hiking and camping skills are described in the *Fieldbook* of the Boy Scouts of America. For more advanced camping skills, Horace Kephart's *Camping and Woodcraft* (Macmillan) is the old standby. Within recent years numerous books on backpacking and canoeing have made their appearance in paperback and hardcover. Ask for them in your local bookstore.

Planning Your Trip

Where do you want to go? That'll be the first thing for you to decide. So study the map of the United States and Canada and select your territory. There are lots of places to choose from—national parks, national forests, wilderness areas, state parks, and provincial parks scattered over the whole continent. For canoeing, certain states and provinces are particularly generously supplied with wilderness lakes and waterways: Maine, Minnesota, New York, Wisconsin; New Brunswick, Ontario, and Quebec.

The next step is to secure topographic maps of the area you have selected for your traveling. For the regular run of topographic maps follow the procedure described on pages 12–13. For traveling in national parks, national forests, and wilderness areas send your request for information to:

National Cartographic Information Center
United States Geological Survey
507 National Center
Reston, Virginia 22092

For trips in state parks write for maps to the Chamber of Commerce or Department of Conservation of the state involved. At the same time, ask for information in regard to camping and canoeing in the area. Many states have special literature with tips for travelers, campers, hunters, and fishermen.

Laying Out Your Route

Now lay out the route you intend to follow through what you consider the most suitable area. Don't be overambitious—a daily stint of around ten miles of hiking or fifteen miles of canoeing is probably all you will care to do if you are in good condition. Don't plan to be on the trail every day of your expedition—schedule certain days for stopovers where you may occupy yourself with your hobby of fishing or hunting or photography or nature study or whatever it happens to be—or for lazying, if that's what you want to do.

Getting Local Information

When you have decided on your route, the time has come to secure local information. In some instances, you may be able to depend on maps alone and on printed information, but conditions often change and you had better make certain of what you can expect before you set out: where equipment may be bought or rented; whether food supplies may be purchased along the route or must be toted from the jumping-off place; what camp sites are available and what the regulations are for their use; whether certain streams are navigable, certain portages passable. You can generally secure this information by dropping a line (with a stamped and self-addressed return envelope) to the "Postmaster" or "General Store" of the village closest to your starting point.

Setting Out

With all preparations taken care of you are ready to set out. And if your qualifications are as good as they ought to be for the kind of trip

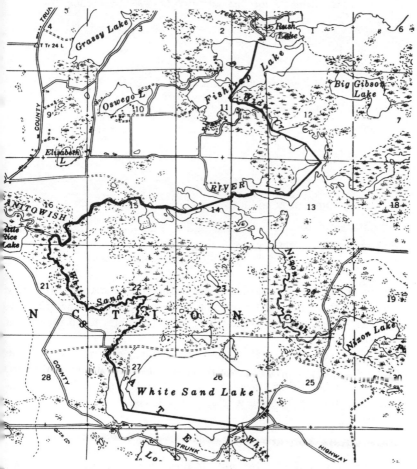

Lay out your tentative canoe route on a topographic map, then secure local information. Straight lines indicate laps traveled by compass.

you have planned you should be able to carry it through with flying colors and have the time of your life.

But there is that little "if."

If for any reason you are not completely positive about your qualifications for an expedition on your own it will pay to set your mind at

Map Symbols for Special WATER FEATURES—Blue

Intermittent lake or pond...

Large rapids...

Small rapids..

Large falls...

Small falls...

Canal, flume, or aqueduct..

Water elevation...*870*

When planning a canoe trip, pay special attention to these map symbols. Rapids are for the trained canoeist only; falls necessitate portaging.

rest by taking along a registered guide for your first trip into a new wilderness area. The next time you come back to the same area you will then have the necessary training and confidence to do the job on your own.

In any event, before setting out on a wilderness trip, provide the local forest ranger or game warden with an itinerary of your trip. Then in case anything unforeseen should happen it will be comparatively easy for the "outside world" to reach you.

Know Where You Are

As you travel along, the most important rule is: *know at all times where you are, according to your map; and know the direction in which you are going, according to your compass.*

Before you set out from one point to the next determine your exact position on the map. Then orient your map and follow map and compass bearings to your next destination. Figure out the distance and the approximate time you should expect to get there. When using the compass, follow the bearing carefully from landmark to landmark.

Check your progress on the map by identifying land features in the terrain on the map whenever possible as you travel. This will assist you in always knowing where you are.

When in Doubt . . .

In spite of all your Orienteering skill there may be times when you feel in doubt about your location or direction. Under such conditions what can you do?

Well, there is one thing you can't do: you can't get lost with a map and a compass in your hands—not if you use your "noodle." *So stop and think.* Take it easy. With a bit of figuring and logical reasoning you should get yourself back on course if you happen to be off:

First of all—did you set your compass bearing correctly from your map? Did you compensate for declination by using a map provided with magnetic-north lines that automatically take care of the declination? If you did, your destination will probably be still ahead of you—your progress was slower than you expected. If you didn't, your destination may be waiting for you somewhere to one side of you—to the right of you in areas of westerly declination; to the left where the declination is easterly.

If you still find yourself stymied, you may decide to return to the last location of which you are positive by following the back-reading of your compass. To do this, travel backward against the direction-of-travel arrow instead of with it, as described on page 78. Even better, if there is a long "catching" landmark ahead of you—a road, a railroad, a river, a lakeshore—you can aim for that and then reschedule your trip from the spot you hit.

Most important—avoid any possibility of going wrong by following to the letter the practices of correct Orienteering: by planning your trip carefully before starting out; by using a map provided with magnetic-north lines; by setting your compass correctly for each stretch of your journey; by studying your map repeatedly to know where you are; by following your compass; and by trusting it to get you to your destination.

"Practice makes master," they say. *Orienteering Practice Makes the Master Orienteer.* The more practice you get, the more certain you become and the less apt you are ever to be in doubt of your location on your trips.

So make it a habit always to bring along compass and map—even on short trips—and take every chance to practice and to experience the joyful sport of Orienteering.

PART IV
Competitive Orienteering

Within comparatively recent years Orienteering as a competitive sport in the form of "Orienteering Races" has swept Europe. Today, with the establishment of national Orienteering Federations in the United States and Canada, it is well on its way to sweeping North America as Orienteering clubs spring up in all states and provinces.

Leaders in outdoor education have found in the different types of competitive Orienteering events a valuable ally in creating a greater interest in all phases of outdoor life, in addition to the mental stimulation these events provide through their demand on skills in using map and compass. The result has been that Orienteering events have become regular features in numerous schools and in many athletic and outdoor clubs. Orienteering events have also become popular in Scouting circles, arranged by Scout councils and by individual Scout and Explorer units.

The word "race" for these types of outdoor events is somewhat of a misnomer. It isn't speed alone that determines the winner in Orienteering; it is a combination of four important things:

> Correct interpretation of instructions
> Careful planning of routes to be followed
> Intelligent use of map and compass
> Time used to cover the entire course

Orienteering is a "thinking sport" in which mental ability supports and often outweighs physical ability. It may be described, as an Australian orienteer has suggested, as "cunning running"—the cunning generally more important than the running.

An especially fast runner may be off to a poor start by failing to follow instructions. Or he may not have studied his map carefully enough when deciding on the best possible route. Or he may be careless in his compass settings and in orienting his map and compass before racing off.

To win an Orienteering race it pays for each participant to start out easy, to spend sufficient time in checking and rechecking, and to figure out the most advantageous procedure. This is especially true for the beginner. By the time a person has caught the Orienteering bug and has become proficient in the sport of Orienteering, his speed will have increased with his skill in using compass and map.

Orienteering as a Sport

An Orienteering race can be fitted into almost any kind of outdoor activity. It can be a special all-day event staged any time of the year for a group of young people or adults. It can be the theme of a day in camp of a Scout troop or an Explorer post or any other kind of camping group, whether boys or girls. An athletic club can use Orienteering races in its physical fitness program. A military unit can combine Orienteering with all types of field work: it is the best method of learning navigation and at the same time building up self-confidence.

An Orienteering race can be an easy activity for untrained or unskilled people of all ages, or it can be developed into a highly competitive event among experts—individuals or teams of two or more. An Orienteering club specifically dedicated to the sport of Orienteering can schedule a string of races of different lengths and varying difficulty for training its members and interested individuals in the intricacies of the sport and for giving them a chance to compete in special events—of local, national, and even international character.

Whatever the event certain requirements must be met:

Suitable Terrain—Preferably the area should be undulating and well-wooded, with several readily identifiable natural or man-made features.

Maps—A topographic map or a map prepared especially for Orienteering should be available for each person or team.

Compasses—An Orienteering compass should be available for each person or team.

Markers—A marker locating each control station should be placed along the course.

Personnel—A sufficient number of persons to be course setters, starters, timers, and other necessary officials should be on hand.

TYPES OF COMPETITIVE ORIENTEERING

Generally speaking, there are two main types of competitive Orienteering events, although each of them adapts itself to much variety:

Point-to-Point Orienteering—The course setter chooses control points in the field for the participants to find but each participant must determine his own route from one known control point to the next.

Preset-Course Orienteering—The course setter not only picks control points in the field for the participants to find but also chooses and presets the routes the participants must follow from one unknown control point to the next throughout the entire course.

Variations of Point-to-Point Orienteering

The most important feature of Point-to-Point Orienteering is the chance it gives the orienteer to make quick decisions and sound choices of routes, based on full knowledge of the proper use of map and compass.

Of the several variations possible of this type, the highly individualistic Cross-Country Orienteering is, by far, the most popular. It is universally used in determining national and international championships.

Two other variations—Score and Relay Orienteering, both involving the free choice of routes, have also attained great popularity. One of the main reasons for this is that, while Cross-Country Orienteering is a personal battle of quickness of mind and physical stamina of each participant against all the others, Score and Relay Orienteering permit team participation of small or even fairly large groups. However, Cross-Country Orienteering can also, under certain circumstances, include team competition—such as, when the three best orienteers from each participating club are considered a team and have their times added together for the team result.

CROSS-COUNTRY ORIENTEERING   OUTDOOR PROJECT

PURPOSE—Test of mental quickness in choosing the best possible routes between controls, and mental agility and physical stamina in following these routes speedily using map and compass.

GROUP PROJECT—The *course setter* chooses on a map suitable terrain for the race, with several readily identifiable natural or man-made features. He then selects 5 to 12 of these features of different degrees of difficulty at varying distances apart (300 to 1,500 feet—100 to 500 meters), forming a more or less circular course 1½ to 2½ miles long (2½ to 4 kilometers) for juniors and beginners; up to 8 to 10 miles (12 to 16 kilometers) for elite orienteers. He visits each control point in the field and determines its exact location on a master map. He then proceeds to develop a course. When determining the order in which the controls should be visited, the course setter

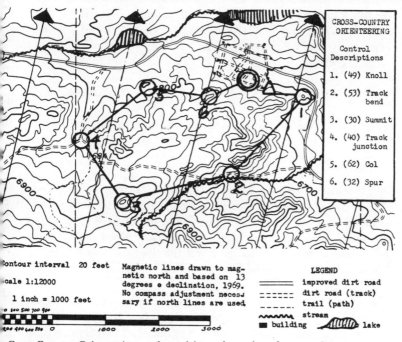

CROSS-COUNTRY
ORIENTEERING

Control
Descriptions

1. (49) Knoll

2. (53) Track
      bend

3. (30) Summit

4. (40) Track
      junction

5. (62) Col

6. (32) Spur

Contour interval 20 feet

cale 1:12000

1 inch = 1000 feet

Magnetic lines drawn to magnetic north and based on 13
degrees e declination, 1969.
No compass adjustment necessary if north lines are used.

LEGEND

═══════ improved dirt road
═ ═ ═ ═ dirt road (track)
─ ─ ─ ─. trail (path)
〰〰〰 stream
■ building   ⏝⏝ lake

Cross-Country Orienteering, each participant determines the routes he wants to follow to reach the control points marked on a master map.

makes Orienteering more interesting and challenging by choosing
controls that offer the participants several route choices. He then
arranges for the production of maps for all participants and prepares
master maps and description lists, describing the nature of the controls. Before the race, he places an Orienteering marker at the exact
location of each control point as indicated on the master map.

The *participants* are provided with the map of the area and the
description list of the controls and are started at one- or two-minute
intervals. For championship events the control points are printed on
the map; for usual events the participants proceed, after having
started, to a master map area where they copy onto their own maps
the control points and the course from the displayed master maps.
Participants then take off to find the controls in the proper sequence
but by routes determined by themselves. Whenever a participant

reaches a control he secures proof of having visited it by marking the proper space on his card with the code symbol of the control. The race is won by the participant who hits all of the control points in the prescribed order and arrives at the finish in the shortest time.

SCORE ORIENTEERING   OUTDOOR PROJECT

PURPOSE—A test of the participants' ability to plan effectively a series of routes, comparing travel time involved, and a test of Orienteering skills in general.

GROUP PROJECT—Score Orienteering differs from Cross-Country Orienteering by the fact that the controls are *not* to be visited in any specified numerical sequence. Instead, each control is given a certain score value. The controls farthest away from the start or the ones most difficult to locate have the highest scores—30 to 50 points. Those close to the start or easiest to find may be valued at 5 to 15 points.

The *course setter* goes about his task exactly as for Cross-Country Orienteering. He selects the control locations and plots them on a master map. But instead of selecting controls to be arranged into a course to be visited in a specific sequence, he picks control locations at random within a radius of one mile from the combined start-and-finish area (thus covering approximately 3 square miles) and picks so many—12 to 30—that no participant could possibly cover all of them within a time limit of, say, 90 minutes. He assigns score points to each control, gives each control a number, and prepares a description list of the controls with their number and score value.

AS INDIVIDUAL COMPETITION—At a pre-start 15 minutes before the actual start, each *participant* is provided with a map of the area and a description list of the controls with their point values indicated. The participant then proceeds to the master map area where he uses the allotted 15 minutes to copy the control locations onto his own map, to decide how many controls he will attempt to reach, and the order in which he desires to visit them. When the pre-start time is up, the participants are started.

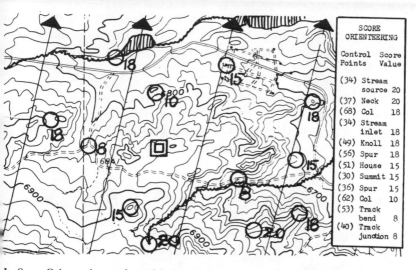

SCORE ORIENTEERING		
Control Points	Score	Value
(34) Stream source		20
(37) Neck		20
(68) Col		18
(34) Stream inlet		18
(49) Knoll		18
(56) Spur		18
(51) House		15
(30) Summit		15
(36) Spur		15
(62) Col		10
(53) Track bend		8
(40) Track junction		8

In Score Orienteering, each participant strives to earn as many score points as possible by hitting the controls that have the highest value.

The objective now is for each participant to score the highest number of points within the time limit. He does this by locating as many control points as possible and marking his control card with their code symbols as proof of having reached them. If he exceeds the time limit, he is penalized by having a certain number of points subtracted from his score—perhaps 1 point for each 10 seconds late—6 points for each minute. A participant arriving at the finish five minutes late will thus have 30 points subtracted from his score. The race is won by the participant who has the highest score after subtracting possible penalty points.

AS TEAM COMPETITION—Score Orienteering adapts itself exceedingly well to team competitions. Such competitions may be handled in different ways:

First Method: Each team member works independently. He decides for himself what controls he wants to reach, sets his own routes, and runs them as an individual, as described above. At the conclusion, after all team members have arrived at the finish, the score may be decided (a) by totaling the scores of all team members and dividing the result by the number of members to come up with an average score, or (b) by totaling the scores of the three highest-scoring participants if the team consists of 3, 4, or 5 members; of the five highest scores if the team consists of 5, 6, 7, or 8 members.

Second Method: A team leader distributes all the control locations among the team members, sending the best orienteers to the farthest or most difficult control locations; the less qualified orienteers are sent to the closest or easiest controls. When all members have returned, the score points of all the controls reached are added up and become the team total.

RELAY ORIENTEERING   OUTDOOR PROJECT

PURPOSE—To use Orienteering for establishing team spirit within a group or club and to further train individual members in the skills of Orienteering.

GROUP PROJECT—Relay Orienteering is Cross-Country Orienteering turned into a team event. As in all other kinds of Orienteering, the *course setter* begins his task by choosing suitable terrain on the map. Next he decides on a central, combined start–change-over–finish area. He then selects a number of control points. The location and arrangement of these controls will depend on the number of members of each team. If there are 3 members to a team, the course may consist of three stages fanning out from the central area

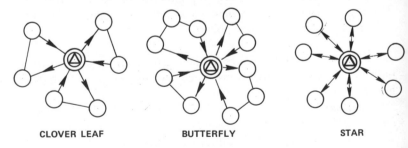

CLOVER LEAF   BUTTERFLY   STAR

The course for Relay Orienteering can assume varying shapes, depending on the number of orienteers to be accommodated.

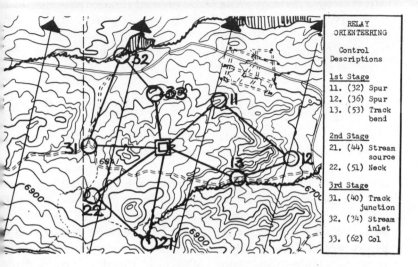

Relay Orienteering is a team competition in which the team members fan out from a central point (double square) to cover several short courses.

in the form of a clover leaf, with each member running a "leaflet" consisting of two or three control points. If 4 members make up a team, the general form of the course may be that of a butterfly, with each team member running one of the four "wings." With 5 to 8 members to a team, the course may be laid out in star form, with each member running a "ray" with a single control. (In a more elaborate relay competition, start and finish may be at two separate places, with change-over stations distributed between them and with the controls forming a circular or linear course.) The controls are set up and the master maps developed in the same way as for Cross-Country Orienteering.

At the start of the race, the first *participant* from each team is given a map and a control-description sheet, then started off. The time is taken for the team. The participant runs to the master map area and copies onto his own map the locations of only those two or three controls that make up his stage. He then takes off to reach the controls and to secure proof of having visited them by marking the team's control card with the code symbols. When he has completed his stage, he turns the control card and map over to the next runner who then runs his stage. And so on until all runners have run their stages. When the last runner finishes, time is taken and the score for the whole team is determined.

The race is won by the team that hits all its assigned controls and arrives at the finish in the shortest time.

WAYFARING   OUTDOOR PROJECT

PURPOSE—To give noncompetitively inclined persons a chance to enjoy the outdoors and the sport of Orienteering at their leisure.

GROUP PROJECT—At an Orienteering event the organizers may open up the easiest course or a special course for young and old who like hiking but who are not particularly interested in the competitive aspects of Orienteering, or are not confident enough in their ability as orienteers. This simple form of Orienteering is particularly suited for families with young children. It provides all participants with an extra challenge beyond the general demands of hiking and gives a feeling of accomplishment as they hit upon the controls along the course.

Participants entering into this leisurely kind of hiking—wayfaring—are provided with a master map of the territory with course and control points indicated. They then take off to follow the course at their own speed, stopping to enjoy the landscape and the beauty of their immediate surroundings whenever they feel like doing so. If they so desire, they can combine their rambling with bird or plant study or with the investigation of various aspects of nature.

While many wayfarers may decide to continue as wayfarers, others may eventually want to get into competitive Orienteering.

Preset-Course Orienteering

Preset-Course Orienteering is a more leisurely type than Point-to-Point. Actually, it is more commonly used and more valuable for training than for competition.

The two main variations of this type—Line Orienteering and Route Orienteering—supplement each other. In Line Orienteering the participant follows a route indicated by a continuous line on the master

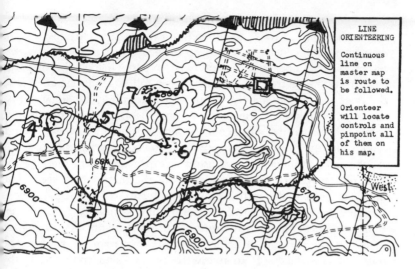

n Line Orienteering, each participant follows a course drawn on a master map. In Route Orienteering, he draws the controls onto his own map.

nap, while in Route Orienteering he is marking on the map the location of the controls he finds in the terrain while following a trail narked with streamers.

Preset Orienteering can also be used to test various outdoor skills not directly related to the use of map and compass as in Project Orienteering or for adding an extra thrill to cross-country skiing as in Ski Orienteering.

LINE ORIENTEERING   OUTDOOR PROJECT

PURPOSE—Test of ability to follow a route indicated on a master map with map and compass.

GROUP PROJECT—The *course setter* proceeds in exactly the same way as for a Cross-Country Orienteering event: he chooses a suitable terrain and selects 5 to 12 control points, forming a more or less circular course but only 2 to 4 miles long. He visits each control, determines its exact location on his map, and puts a numbered control marker on it. From this moment on the picture changes: instead of marking the control locations on the master map, the course setter presets the course to be followed by drawing on the map the exact route he desires the participants to follow from one control to the next around the course. Some of the legs may be along paths, roads, streams, lakeshores, which can be followed by map alone, while others may be cross-country legs on direct bearings through woods and over fields which can be followed only by compass.

At the starting point the *participants* are provided with maps of the area and then started off at intervals to the master map area. The intervals need to be rather long to prevent one participant from stepping on the heels of the one before him—possibly 3, 4, or even 5 minutes, depending on the number of participants. At the master map area the participant copies onto his own map the route to be followed then takes off to follow it by map and compass. If the route is followed correctly, the participant will pass all the control points in numerical order. His task now is to plot exactly the point on his map where each control is located, circle the map location with pencil or pen, and note the code symbol of the marker on his score card.

Normally, time has no bearing on the winning of this type of Orienteering, but a *time limit* for completing the race should be announced in advance.

The winner is the participant who has found the most stations and has plotted them correctly on his map.

PROJECT ORIENTEERING   OUTDOOR PROJECT

PURPOSE—To test, in addition to following a route indicated on a master map, other outdoor skills of the participants.

GROUP PROJECT—The *course setter* sets up a route exactly as for Line Orienteering. On the day of the event each control is manned with a project official who informs the participants of the project to be performed and scores them for their performance. Such project may be related to Orienteering: Landmark Hunt (pages 58–59), for instance, or Find the Bearings (pages 73–74). Or the project may involve camping and Scoutcraft skills: "Make a fire with two matches"; "Collect a single leaf from each of ten different trees"; "Make a simple bridge and cross the brook"—and so on.

The *participants* may work as individuals, as buddy teams, or in small groups, such as a Scout patrol. They proceed as for Line Orienteering, performing the different projects at the controls.

The winner is the participant or team that has the highest total score for the various projects, including a score for a map with correctly plotted controls.

ROUTE ORIENTEERING   OUTDOOR PROJECT

PURPOSE—To test the ability to plot on a map the location of controls the participants pass when they follow a trail marked with streamers.

GROUP PROJECT—The *course setter* prepares the event basically the same way as for Cross-Country Orienteering and Line Orienteering. The event is ideal for beginners, as nobody can get lost! The distance should be kept within 1 to 3 miles. When the course setter has established the course, he follows it and marks it by tying colored streamers—plastic or cloth—onto trees, fence posts, and other objects at such distances apart that from wherever a streamer is displayed the next can be seen along the route. The course should preferably follow trails, creekbeds, ridges, or other clear landmarks. With a distance between the controls of 800 to 1,200 feet, the course setter places control markers along the route.

At the starting point, the *participants* are provided with maps of the area and then started off at one- or two-minute intervals to follow the clearly marked course. The task of each participant is to follow the course on his map all of the time, so he knows where he is. When he comes to a control marker, he circles the location on the map as exactly as possible.

The winner is the participant who turns in his map with the most correctly marked controls. Any mistakes cause a deduction of, for instance, 2 points for every $1/16$ inch of error from a total of 100 points for all controls correctly marked. Time taken for the route may also be counted as a factor in deciding the winner. If so, the penalty for incorrectly marked controls could be 2 minutes for every $1/16$ inch of error.

The participants also can be asked to draw the entire course on their maps as they follow it. In that case, if two or more participants end with the same number of points, the winner will be the one with the most correctly drawn route.

SKI ORIENTEERING   OUTDOOR PROJECT

PURPOSE—To add spice to regular cross-country skiing by combining skiing with the skills of Orienteering.

GROUP PROJECT—The *course setter* proceeds with the preparations in the same way as for that type of foot Orienteering he has chosen for his event. The most simple Ski Orienteering events to organize are Line Orienteering and Route Orienteering, as there are no special problems. But to organize Cross-Country Orienteering on skis some special preparations may be necessary.

A suitable terrain for Cross-Country Ski Orienteering is quite different from that usable for Cross-Country Orienteering on foot: the best terrain is a cultivated area with a great number of tracks and trails. And here is where the difficulties in organizing and preparation may come in. If not enough tracks and trails are available, the course setter may have to arrange to have more added, using a snowmobile or a team of five or more skiers for the purpose. All tracks and trails—existing or specially made—must then be clearly indicated on all of the maps. Depending on the terrain, the snow conditions, and the participants' skiing ability, the course may be from 3 to 10 miles long. The control points should be few and easy to locate for the skier when he arrives in their vicinity: the basis of competition should be route choice and not a frantic final search for the control. Controls should be located at fixed and clearly visible features of the landscape on or fairly close to the tracks.

At the starting point the *participants* are provided with maps of the area with course and control points already included. They are started at 2- to 3-minute intervals. As in foot Orienteering the task of each participant is to follow the course, locate the controls, and return within a certain time limit. The winner is the participant who has located all controls and has returned to the finish in the shortest time. If a participant misses a control, he may be penalized either by disqualification or by adding 10–20 minutes for each missed control, depending on the degree of difficulty and the length of the course. Those who have located all controls should, independently of time, be placed ahead of those with penalty points for missed controls.

Other Varieties

Almost all Orienteering events described here can be run with different means of travel through the landscape. There are events organized for canoeists, bicyclists, and horseback riders.

Other varieties of Orienteering than those described in this book are also possible. Your own imagination is the limit.

YOUR FIRST ORIENTEERING RACE

After you have indulged in your own private Orienteering for a while, alone or with friends, the day will come when you feel so competent in the skills of using map and compass that you will want to prove your ability in competition with others interested in the sport of Orienteering. And so you try to find out if, by chance, an Orienteering club already exists in your locality. If you have no luck finding one, drop a line to your respective national Orienteering Federation at the address stated on page 210. You will receive information on clubs that may exist in your vicinity, or suggestions on how to get one started. Keep in mind that the sport is young on this continent and a club should be looked upon as "local" for you even if the headquarters are 30 to 50 miles or more away. That's the distance you may have to travel anyway to get to a good Orienteering area. If there is a club nearby, contact it for information on its programs. Shortly afterwards you will receive the club's bulletin with announcements of meetings

and events. Study the bulletin carefully and note specifically the up-
coming event, which may appear as follows:

Saturday, September 15th – Cross-Country Orienteering Events – Open
to members and non-members

AREA: Pound Ridge Reservation. Participants will be informed of
actual starting point one week before events.

EVENTS: White Course, approx. 1-2 miles, for beginning orienteers
Yellow Course, approx. 2-3 miles, for budding orienteers
Red Course, approx. 4-6 miles, for advanced orienteers

FIRST PARTICIPANTS AWAY: 10:30 a.m.

ENTRY FEE: Seniors $1.00 – Juniors $.50

ENTRIES: Before September 5th to
P. Jones, Secretary, 1234 South Road, Pound Ridge

Notice that the club offers three courses of varying difficulty: a
"white" course for beginning, a "yellow" course for budding, and a
"red" course for advanced orienteers. You will need to learn what
"competitive Orienteering" is all about, so you sign up for the easiest
course, the "white" one.

A few days later you receive a post card from the club's secretary:

THIRD ORIENTEERING RACE OF THE NONESUCH ORIENTEERING CLUB

DATE: Saturday, September 15th, 10:00 a.m.
MEET: Enter Pound Ridge Reservation at North Gate. Turn right
onto improved dirt road. Proceed to reception area.
Park in space indicated by signs.
DRESS: Long pants recommended. Brambles in spots, poison ivy
in others. If shorts preferred, wear long stockings.
EQUIPMENT: Bring Orienteering compass, red ball-point pen for
marking map, plastic bag for map, wristwatch, bag lunch.
STARTING TIME: Your starting time is 11:02 a.m. Please report to
registration desk not later than 20 minutes before.
SPECIAL NOTE: Permission for trespass secured from all property owners. Only conditions: 1. Positively no smoking –
much down-timber. 2. No crossing of cultivated fields.

P. Jones, Secretary

Here you have the basic information. For clothing you settle on a pair of old work pants and a long-sleeved shirt. You pick your lightest hiking shoes—you don't expect to break any speed records but still don't want to be left too far behind. The equipment is easy: you bring out your Silva® compass, get a plastic bag from the kitchen closet, buy a red ball-point pen (if you don't already have one). The watch is already on your wrist, and it will take only a minute to make up a bag lunch on the morning of the event.

Starting Procedure

The day arrives. You take off from home in plenty of time, arrive at your destination, and park your car next to dozens of others—some of them with out-of-state license plates. You walk to the assembly area. Scores of other orienteers are there already, some of them in special Orienteering suits, or track suits, others in hiking clothes. You approach the reception desk and are greeted like a long-lost friend. The receptionist gives you a control card with your name and starting time already filled in (see page 200). You are informed that you will be "called up" three minutes before your start. In some events, you may receive a "bib" with a number on it for easier timing of the runners.

You turn away from the reception desk to make room for other entrants, then look around. Things are really beginning to move. The orienteers are walking in the direction of the starting area. This particular club has set up a nine-foot by nine-foot starting grid, divided into three-foot squares by ropes pegged into the ground.

You hear a whistle blast. The three orienteers standing in the front row of the grid take off. Those in the two other rows advance, and the last row is filled with three more participants. You soon find out what this is all about.

At 10:59 A.M.—three minutes before your starting time—the "call-up" official calls three numbers: yours and the numbers of two others. You step into one of the last-row squares. You are in a "Get in!" square. You notice the control cards in the hands of your neighbors: one is red—he is signed up for the "red" course—the other is yellow for the "yellow" course.

A minute passes. There is another blast on the whistle. The front row participants run off, and you and your neighbors move into the "Get ready!" line. Here you are presented with a slip of paper with typewriting on it. You scan it quickly:

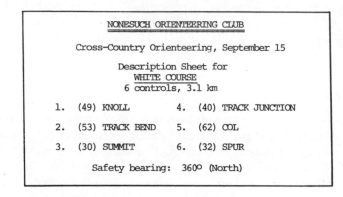

NONESUCH ORIENTEERING CLUB

Cross-Country Orienteering, September 15

Description Sheet for
WHITE COURSE
6 controls, 3.1 km

1. (49) KNOLL   4. (40) TRACK JUNCTION

2. (53) TRACK BEND   5. (62) COL

3. (30) SUMMIT   6. (32) SPUR

Safety bearing: 360° (North)

Those are the six points in the landscape that you are supposed to find on the "white" course. The official giving you the slip impresses you with the admonition that the controls must be visited in the exact order indicated and that their code symbols must be punched in the proper square of your control card with the pin punch or clipper found at the controls. The numbers in brackets are the numbers found on the actual control markers in the field. They provide a double check that you are at the right control point.

One more minute. The whistle blows again. The front-row runners disappear and you and your neighbors move into the "Get set!" line. Here you receive a map of the area in which the "white" course is laid. (You will find a reduced reproduction of this map on page 143.) You take a quick look at it: scale 1 inch to 1,000 feet; contour intervals 20 feet. You praise the organizers for having provided a map with magnetic north-south lines—you had expected that you would have had to draw them in yourself the way you did when you went Orienteering on your own (page 115). The fellow next to you suggests that you tip off the top of each magnetic line with a red arrow so there will be no question in your mind where north lies on your map.

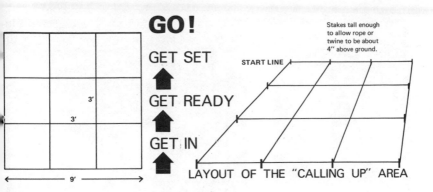

GO!

GET SET

▲

GET READY

▲

GET IN

▲

Stakes tall enough
to allow rope or
twine to be about
4" above ground.

START LINE

LAYOUT OF THE "CALLING UP" AREA

3'

3'

← 9' →

A popular layout for the calling-up area consists of a nine-foot square divided with ropes into three-foot squares in which the orienteers take their places.

The last minute is up. At last you hear the whistle blast you have been waiting for: "Go!"

The Master Maps

On the first stretch you use neither map nor compass: colored streamers lead you to the master-map area, the actual starting point. The white streamers bring you to the master map that will indicate the "white" course. These maps—one or more for each class—are mounted on pieces of plywood. The master map for your particular course is given on page 143.

On the master map, the master-map area where you now find your-self is indicated by a triangle. Each control point you are to visit is circled—5 mm in diameter—in red ink. The circles are numbered and connected in numerical order by straight red lines. Your immediate job is to copy the circles, the numbers, and the lines onto your own map as precisely as possible. The position of each circle is critical: the control marker is situated in its exact center.

When you have finished copying, you slip the map and description list into the plastic bag you brought and fold it so that not much more than the first leg of the course shows.

A special red-and-white prism-shaped marker indicates the exact location of each control point. A pin punch or stamp is used to mark the control card.

The Race

You are ready now to run the first leg—from the master-map area to control "1. (49) Knoll." This should be easy: it is a short straight distance on fairly level ground, close to and parallel to a road.

You first orient your map to familiarize yourself with map and terrain. You take a quick look around, then set your Orienteering compass for the bearing and take off. You see the road to the left almost all the time. It helps to give you confidence. And there is the red-and-white marker. You see it from about fifty feet away. When you reach it, you check its number against the number on your control card, pick up the special pin punch that is attached to it by a cord, and use it for making the code symbol on your card in square 1.

Now for control 2. You study the map. This looks like a toughie. The direct beeline would take you up and over a hill of seven contour intervals: 140 feet. You remember from your earlier Orienteering the

The exciting start of an Orienteering race: At the signal, the orienteers in the front line of the starting grid take off.

Busy in master map area transferring control points to own maps.

After deciding on a route, young and old race off for the first control.

admonition "There's always another way." You look for it. Sure enough: there is an improved road a short distance to the east of you—you can follow it south until you hit the dirt road, then continue west until you arrive at control "2. (53) Track bend." You quickly start jogging along. There's nothing to it. After getting onto the road, you need neither map nor compass—you simply remember what to do.

From 2 to control "3. (30) Summit" you wonder whether you should continue along the road, then strike north at an appropriate spot. You give it up: there are no landmarks on your map to determine the "appropriate spot" from which to get off the road. So you set your compass and take off on the bearing up an incline, then across a fairly flat plateau covered with pines and fallen trees here and there. You find the control, check its number, and punch your card.

From 3 to "4. (40) Track junction," you notice that the beeline would take you down one contour interval and up another. What different route might be better? It only takes you a moment to discover that the easiest route is southwest on the contour to the road, then along the road westward first, then northward to the junction. That's the route you follow. No problem locating control 4.

The next two controls—"5. (62) Col" and "6. (32) Spur"—you decide to take on straight compass. You reach them without any special difficulty beyond having to run through a couple of stretches of undergrowth that cut down your speed.

Finish Procedure

At control 6 you have reached the last control of the "white" course. It is all over, except for the final spurt toward the Finish. The route home from the last control point is marked with colored streamers. You jog along the marked trail until you see the "FINISH" banner ahead, then pick up speed to arrive in the style of a real orienteer.

You turn in your control card. An official writes on it your time of finishing and figures out the time elapsed. Another official checks the clipper marks: the six spaces are clipped correctly and in the right order.

The control point has been reached. Now the control card is marked.

A quick check with compass on map and it is off to the next control!

The finish of a national Orienteering event. The orienteers race full speed along the marked route to the finish line, applauded by the spectators.

You mingle with the orienteers who have already finished their courses. They are telling each other how they made out and are comparing notes on the way they hit the different control points.

The results of the races are put up. No, you didn't come out the winner. But you weren't at the bottom of the list either. You are quite satisfied with yourself. You have had your first injection of the thrill of competitive Orienteering. You make up your mind that Orienteering is the sport for you. And so you sign on the dotted line and join the Nonesuch Orienteering Club.

HINTS ON COMPETITIVE ORIENTEERING

As you get deeper and deeper into competitive Orienteering and take part in races of varying difficulty, you will be picking up a number of special techniques that elite orienteers use to come in winners. In addition to developing an easy energy-saving running style, these techniques involve the most effective way of choosing the routes between controls and in following them with greatest precision.

Choosing Your Routes

Your route choosing starts while you are still copying the control points and the beelines between them onto your own map in the master-map area. As you do so, you get a general mental picture of the course as a whole and of the landscape through which you will be traveling, and you begin to formulate your procedure.

It is now a matter of determining the quickest and least exhausting route from one control point to the next—a route that in the end will lead you with certainty to the control you are supposed to reach.

The choice of the right route may determine whether you win or lose the race. And so, before making a blind stab at arriving at a route, you seek the answers to three important questions:

"From what direction will I attack the control?"

"What helps will I have in reaching it?"

"What obstacles will be in my way?"

Attack Points

Controls are rarely placed on prominent features of the landscape. On the contrary. A clever course setter will probably choose control points that can only be reached by final precision Orienteering: a small knoll, for instance, or the saddle between two low hills, the spur on the side of a hill, the source of a small stream.

The problem of determining from what direction to take the control can most easily be solved by going backward: by first studying the immediate vicinity of the control for a prominent landscape feature that can be fairly easily reached and definitely identified.

Such a feature, used for a direct approach to a control, is known in Orienteering parlance as an attack point. An attack point may be a road crossing, a stream junction, a bridge, a house, or any other feature clearly shown on the map and reasonably easy to find.

After selecting a feasible attack point, the next step is for you to study the map for all possible routes that will lead you to it and to decide whether to follow the beeline drawn on your map or whether a route to the left or the right of the direct line may be more advantageous by offering more assists and fewer obstacles.

Assists in the Field

There are usually a great number of special features shown on your map that will assist you in your route choice and will help you reach your selected attack point.

Handrails—A handrail is a long feature that runs more or less parallel to the direction in which you are supposed to go.

A road or path is, of course, the most obvious handrail. A power line or a telephone line through the landscape is perfect. So is a fence or a railroad.

A handrail may also take the form of a natural feature, such as the edge of a field or clearing or a ridge or a valley. A fast-moving stream may do the trick; a slow-moving stream is less desirable—its windings may throw you off your direction. Even two hilltops in the distance, lined up in the direction you want to go, may act as a handrail.

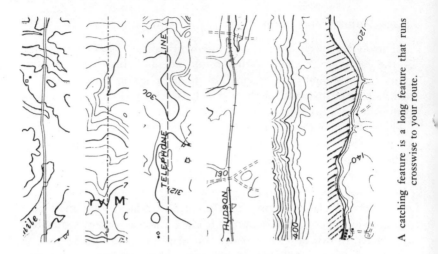

A handrail is a long feature that runs more or less parallel to the direction in which you are supposed to go.

Your least obvious handrail, but one of the most helpful ones, is the sun. Don't overlook it as a most valuable direction pointer once you have your direction established. In open terrain, you can use the sun in your face; with the sun in back of you, you can follow your own shadow. Even at a side angle, the sun can give you assistance in retaining your set direction. In wooded areas with occasional open spaces, you can use the shadows cast by the trees in the same fashion.

Keep in mind that the position of the sun is constantly changing, so you may have to adjust your use of the sun or the shadows as you move along, especially on longer distances.

Catching Features—A catching feature—or collecting feature—is a long feature that runs more or less crosswise to your route. Here, also, man-made highways or roads, power lines or telephone lines will assist you. So will natural features such as rivers and lakes.

When you know that there is a long feature ahead that will catch you and then guide you left or right toward the attack point, you can run rough Orienteering at full speed with less frequent map and compass checks.

Checkpoints—To be on the safe side, the route you finally decide on should have a reasonable number of checkpoints that will assure you that you are actually on the chosen route. Such checkpoints should be conspicuous features that are clearly indicated on your map.

The same kind of feature that will make a good attack point at the end of the route to the control will make a good checkpoint along the route. But there will be many others: the cliff that should be at your right for part of the route; the pond that should be coming up on your left; the bend in the road where you are to leave the road to run cross-country; the spot where the power line crosses the highway—and many others.

Overcoming Obstacles

In choosing your route from one control point to the next, you will find that the straight line is not always the best for saving time and energy. As a matter of fact, the course setter will have seen to it that there are obstacles in your way that will force you to a choice of routes. Such obstacles may be hills or valleys, forests or bog land, lakes or marshes, cliffs or quarries. You will need to make up your mind quickly whether to tackle the obstacle straight on or to choose a route around it, whether to pick a route that is short but tough or another that is longer but easier.

Over or Around?—There is nothing quite so tiring and time consuming as climbing a hill or a mountain, as opposed to running on level ground. So before climbing check the elevation of the obstacle in front of you and decide if it will be better to run a detour around it.

Expert orienteers have reached the conclusion that for every contour interval of 20 feet they have to climb—the vertical distance of each interval on your 1:24,000 map—they expend the time and energy equivalent to running 250 feet on the level in addition to the direct horizontal distance shown on the map.

Let us say that on the leg to your next control, you run up against a hill that rises 80 feet—four contour intervals—with a horizontal distance of 300 feet. Using the formula you arrive at four times 250 feet, plus 300 feet—a total of 1,300 feet. Obviously a detour of less than that distance—say, 1,000 feet—should work to your advantage—provided, of course, that you will have no difficulty locating the next control on the other side of the hill.

If you are a good runner but only a fair climber, you might want to take the detour contouring around the hill—that is, keeping yourself at the same contour elevation. If you are a good climber you would go straight up and over. Most expert orienteers would probably make the climb unless the face of the hill or mountain was exceptionally steep or the route around not much longer.

Through or Around?—It isn't just the elevation you have to think about in your progress: the vegetation you encounter also needs to be considered. Should you be faced with dense forest or areas covered with brambles, or tall grass, or semi-open forest with a light undergrowth, you may want to study your map for the possibility that roads and trails surrounding the area may bring you more quickly to your destination.

So, during your training for competitive Orienteering, find out how long it takes you to cover a certain distance—say, 1,000 feet—along roads and paths and through various kinds of vegetation. Let's say you arrive at something like the following:

Terrain	Time to cover 1,000 feet	Ratio	Distance covered in 2 minutes
Roads and paths	2 minutes	1	1,000 feet
Tall grass	4 minutes	2	500 feet
Forest with light underbrush	6 minutes	3	333 feet
Dense forest or bramble area	8 minutes	4	250 feet

By comparing the time needed for running through dense forest toward your destination with the time it will take you to reach it by roads and paths, you will see that for each 250 feet through dense forest, you will be better off on roads and paths as long as the distance is less than four times as long; that is, less than 1,000 feet. Similarly,

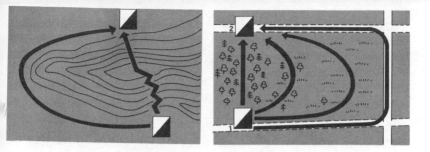

When you meet an obstacle such as a hill, you must decide whether to go over or around. If the obstacle is a forest, the question is, "Through or around?"

you will shave one-third off time and energy by running across grassland rather than running through forest with light undergrowth.

Definitely Around—Obstacles you must definitely plan to go around are: ponds and lakes, swamps and bogs, new plantations and cultivated fields, outcrops and restricted areas (private property).

If you can see across the obstacle, simply pick a prominent feature on the other side—a large tree, a boulder, a house—in the compass direction toward the next control. Then run around the obstacle until you hit the landmark and follow the bearing still set on your compass.

If the obstacle is large and clearly marked on the map—such as a lake—you might get around it by striking out for one end of it and then taking a new direct bearing from the end point of the obstacle toward your control point.

Finalizing the Route

With a suitable attack point considered and with full awareness of all assists and obstacles ahead of you, you can now decide on the route you want to follow. For quick reference, you may want to indicate it on your map with a thin line of your red ball-point pen.

Make up your mind to stick to the route in a general way, but be flexible enough to make whatever changes may be necessary to solve special problems you may encounter.

Following Your Routes

You have decided on the route to the next control. You are off!

If you are a golfer, you may now think of what lies ahead as a game of golf: first the bold whack that will send the ball off the tee in the direction of the fairway; next, getting the ball onto the green and as close to the hole as possible; finally, the precise putt that will send the ball into the hole.

An even better analogy is the "traffic light" principle adopted by most elite orienteers. The principle here is the same as in driving a car. If a green light is ahead, you drive on at full, safe speed. Yellow tells you to slow down and proceed with care. At red, you roll up to the line and come to a halt. Using this method you will judge the difficulty of the different segments, grade the segments into green, yellow, and red, and proceed accordingly:

Green segment (rough Orienteering)—This is the first part of the leg that takes you from your present location toward a catching feature or along a handrail in the direction of the next control or checkpoint along the route. To cover this stretch you will use *rough Orienteering* and run at full speed.

Yellow segment (standard Orienteering)—You have reached the catching feature and now have to locate the attack point that will bring you close to the next control. You keep a fairly good speed and go in for *standard Orienteering* by map and compass, keeping track of distance traveled.

Red segment (precision Orienteering)—The final part of the leg, from attack point to control, requires *precision Orienteering:* exact map reading, precision setting and following of compass, accurate measuring of distance on map with accurate pace counting to match.

Under certain conditions it may well happen that you have to switch temporarily from "Green" to "Yellow" or "Red" and vice versa in your travel and navigation between two control points. But the normal development would be from "Green" to "Yellow" to "Red"—and there is the control!

Rough Orienteering for the Green Segment

Rough Orienteering is the method used for moving quickly toward a catching feature or to an easy-to-find checkpoint. It involves rough map reading and rough compass setting and following.

Set the compass on the map for the bearing to the next control or to the attack point you intend to use. Before taking the compass off the map, orient the map, pointing the line for the route to be followed in the correct direction. Finally, orient yourself—face the direction you are to go.

Rough Compass—Hold the compass at waist height in the usual way and turn yourself until the compass is oriented, with the north part of the needle lying directly over the north-pointing arrow of the compass housing. Your compass is ready to act as your steering instrument, guiding you along a straight route in the field.

Raise your eyes and look far ahead for a prominent steering mark in the exact direction in which the direction-of-travel arrow points: a big tree, a large boulder, a hilltop in the distance, a spire, a TV tower, or what-not. You then take off at full speed toward the steering mark. Beyond the first steering mark, aim for another in the direction you want to go. Continue running, checking your compass only once in a while, slowing down just enough to let the needle come to rest.

You may have planned your route to hit a handrail along the way. In that case, shift your attention from the compass to the handrail and proceed toward the catching feature.

Whenever you reach a checkpoint, stop long enough to orient your map and to check whether to continue on the planned route or to reconsider your decision. Then reset the compass on the map for the next bearing. When you become an expert orienteer, you may not even place the compass on the map for doing the job: you simply judge the next bearing by comparing the route line with the magnetic north-south lines on the map, twist the compass housing to the appropriate number of degrees, orient yourself to the compass direction, and run the next stretch.

Rough Map Reading—While running on the compass, check the map from time to time to make certain that the landscape picture in front of you coincides with what you see on the map and to make sure that you reach the checkpoints along the route—that the cliff that is supposed to be at your right and the lake to the left are actually there and are being passed according to plan. So you will know at all times exactly where you are, keep the map oriented by inspection and, as needed, by compass, and let your thumb follow the route on the map.

Keeping your map oriented necessitates that you shift its position in your hand each time you change a direction along the route. If your direction is north, all printing will read right-side-up. If you are running south, the printing will be upside-down. If west or east, the printing will line up with the direction in which you are going. Get into the habit of always keeping the map oriented when you read it. Ignore the printing, since names and other texts have little importance when you are out in the field Orienteering.

For rough map reading do not bother about details. Get a general idea of the landscape, with emphasis on prominent features. Follow, in the main, the route you have decided on, changing it only to overcome particular obstacles or local situations that may arise.

Aiming Off—Controls are often established in the vicinity of a spot where a catching feature is met or crossed by another feature. It may be placed, for instance, close to where a small stream runs into a larger one or where a path joins a road. In such cases the actual juncture would be a logical attack point. But to locate the juncture you need to know at what point to hit the catching feature so that you will not be running toward the right when the juncture is to the left, or vice versa.

To assure this, make use of an Orienteering technique known as "aiming off." In this, instead of aiming directly at the exact location of the juncture, you aim off your compass by setting it toward a point 100 or 200 feet (30 to 60 meters) to the right or left of it, depending on its character and the distance to it. The longer the distance, the more you aim off to be safe.

When using joining streams as a catching feature, aim off slightly upstream: when you hit the stream, you will then know that you have to run downstream to find the river junction near which the control is located. In the case of joining roads, you may aim right or left as you

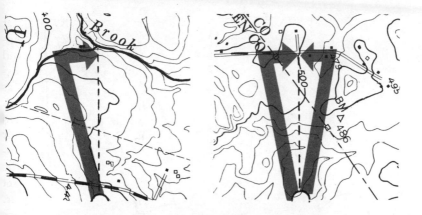

In aiming off toward a stream juncture, aim off upstream and follow stream downstream to juncture. Aim off left or right for a road juncture.

prefer: you will then find the road juncture by going left if you aimed right or by going right if you aimed left.

Standard Orienteering for the Yellow Segment

After running full speed through the green segment of your route, you reach a point where you realize that more care is needed. An imaginary yellow light is flashing and demands that you make more exact use of the Orienteering skills you have learned. It is a matter of locating and passing all the checkpoints you have on your map that lead you in the right direction.

Standard Map and Compass Reading—From the very beginning you have been running with your map oriented so that you had a general idea of the landscape in front of you. Now you need to follow your progress from checkpoint to checkpoint with greater care.

Fold your map so the immediate part of the leg you are running will show. Place your thumb on the map, with your nail pointing in the direction you want to go, in such a way that your nail edge is precisely over the spot where you are now standing. As you proceed, check every point you pass on the route and move your thumb so that

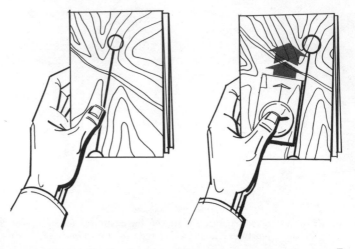

Orienteers use map-reading-by-thumb to follow their progress on the map. For even more exactness you can use the map-reading-by-compass-corner method.

its place on the map is always where you are on the route. This method—"map-reading-by-thumb"—is the most effective kind of map reading. It permits a sharper analysis of the terrain ahead and reduces the risk of error.

To save time some orienteers combine map-reading-by-thumb with the process of using the compass. After the compass has been set for the proper bearing they carry compass and map in the same hand, holding them firmly together, with the edge of the compass lined up with the route on the map, the direction-of-travel arrow pointing forward. They then keep compass and map and themselves oriented by always keeping the north part of the compass needle over the north arrow of the compass housing. By this arrangement, the front right-hand or left-hand corner of the base plate takes the place of the thumb, thus, in a way, turning map-reading-by-thumb into "map-reading-by-compass-corner." As you proceed, slide the compass over the map, always keeping the corner at your location. When the route changes direction, simply shift the compass and reset the housing to the magnetic lines.

With the compass set, follow the bearing in the usual way, by aiming for steering marks along the bearing. In rough compass work in the green segment you should have been able to check a bearing on the compass while running, but in the yellow phase, you need to stop to let the needle come to an absolute rest for a positive bearing.

Pace Counting—If the spaces between the checkpoints in a yellow segment become tricky, with too many details or too few, it may be necessary for you to measure distances on the map and to pace count these distances in the field.

With a little practice you will soon learn to judge long distances in the field. If you have drawn the magnetic north-south lines on your map at one-inch intervals, you know that the distance from a feature on one line on the 1:24,000 map to a feature at a right angle to it on the next line is 2,000 feet in the field. Half the distance between two lines would be 1,000 feet; one-quarter of the distance 500 feet. If yours is a 1:12,000 map, the distance between two lines would be 1,000 feet in the field. Your thumb may actually be one inch wide and the distance it would cover would be 2,000 or 1,000 feet respectively.

For shorter distances and for more exact measurements, you will need to use the inch- or centimeter-rule that is engraved on the front edge or on the side of the base plate of your Orienteering compass.

But whether you measure by one method or another you still have to translate the number of feet arrived at into steps or, better, into paces, that is, double-steps, which you count each time you put your left foot (or right foot) to the ground.

You have probably already determined the length of your pace in walking on a level road, as described on page 53. For advanced Orienteering you will need to know the length of your pace over various terrain and at different slopes.

If the distance between two checkpoints is 400 feet and the length of your walking pace 5 feet, you know that 80 paces of walking will cover the distance. But the minute you run uphill or downhill the length of your pace will change and the number of steps to be taken will be different.

If you have tested your pace, you will know the difference. If you haven't, the following table will give you an idea of the number of places for covering certain terrain features by the general kind of jog-running commonly used in Orienteering:

Terrain	*Number of paces for 100 feet*	*Number of paces for 100 meters*
Level road or path	15	50
Grassland or meadow	17	56
Open forest	20	66
Dense forest	25	83
Uphill (depending on slope)	30+	100+
Downhill (depending on slope)	10−	35−

In other words, you will be taking twice as many paces going uphill as you will on a level road, but one-third fewer going downhill.

When you become a skilled orienteer, you will learn to take your measurements in terms of paces instead of feet. If you are mathematically minded, you can do this arithmetically by measuring map distances by inches or centimeters, translating them into feet or meters, and dividing the result by the length of your pace. Or you may do what a lot of smart orienteers do: develop a pace scale for running on level ground which you can glue onto the front edge of the base plate of your compass and thus save yourself a lot of figuring. Such pace scales for map scales 1:10,000, 1:15,000, and 1:20,000 would look like this if made for a person with a pace length of 42 to 43 paces for 330 feet (100 meters):

These scales give the number of paces to take for a measured distance on the map under average terrain conditions. Adjustments will have to be made for rougher or more easily traveled routes, or you can have an additional pace scale, either for very rough terrain or for easily run trails or open terrain, glued to the other side of the compass plate.

The basic idea has been developed and copyrighted in Norway by

Willy Lorentzen. This does not prohibit you from making your own pace scale.

Precision Orienteering for the Red Segment

The part of your route from the attack point to the control is the most critical segment of your journey. The imaginary warning light is definitely *flashing red*. Your success in reaching the control now depends on the way you practice precision Orienteering, with full attention to precision map reading, precision compass setting and following, and precision measuring and pace counting.

Precision Map Reading—As you approach the control it becomes imperative for you to know exactly where you are for every pace you move ahead. This will require that you match even more checkpoints in the field with their symbols on your map and make even more intensive use of the map-reading-by-thumb method.

To do this reading correctly, you have to slow down. The seconds spent in precision map reading will be amply repaid by the accuracy with which you can move toward the control. For the final distance to the control it may be necessary—or safest, anyway—to depend entirely on the compass, especially if the control is located on a small terrain feature.

Precision Compass Setting and Following—Precision costs time—but even elite orienteers are willing to pay the time it costs for taking the last critical compass bearings and for following them exactly.

To set the compass for complete accuracy you will most certainly want to follow the example of the experts and come to a complete halt for the moment it will take you to hold the compass firmly on the map and twist the housing to the precise bearing.

Similarly, to follow the compass with precision, you will also halt completely for the few seconds it takes for the compass needle to come to rest.

Precision Measuring and Pace Counting—One more thing is yet required. Before you continue toward the control measure the exact distance to the control and quickly translate the measurement into paces. By doing so you will know the spot where the control should be found so that you will not, by chance, overshoot the mark.

With precise knowledge of the map features, precise setting of your compass, precise number of paces determined, you can proceed with confidence and speed directly to the control.

And there it is: the terrain point with the red-and-white marker you have striven so hard to reach. Quickly check the code number of the marker to make sure that it coincides with the code number (in parentheses) on your description sheet. It does. Stamp or clip or punch your card with the code symbol of the control, orient your map, and reset compass for the next leg, and take off.

And so on, until the FINISH banner tells you that you have completed the race.

The Post Mortem

As soon as you are checked in, you mingle with other orienteers who have completed the same course and take part in a friendly *post mortem* discussion.

Here you have a chance to compare the routes you chose with the routes chosen by others. Each orienteer will point out what he considered advantages of the routes he decided on compared with the advantages and disadvantages of other routes.

Such discussions will be of great value to you in future Orienteering efforts. You will have a chance to evaluate each route selection from all points of view and you will pick up hints, information, and pointers that might have otherwise escaped your attention.

ORGANIZING AN ORIENTEERING EVENT

The organizing and running of an Orienteering event depends on the scope of it; a simple event can be handled by a couple of interested people, while a large event will require a more complex organization and a dozen or more officials with clearly defined duties.

Staging a Minor Orienteering Event

It happens quite frequently that an enthusiast who has learned his Orienteering elsewhere takes the initiative for staging a small event and more or less takes care of all details himself, from course setting and map preparation to handling start and finish arrangements. In your own case you may decide to organize an easy Orienteering event for family or neighbors, or for a Scout troop or other youth group, and run it with the help of a couple of friends. To do it most effectively, study the pages that follow, describing the staging of a standard event, then use your own judgment in determining the number of helpers you need and what their duties will be, combining the responsibilities into as few hands as possible.

Staging a Standard Orienteering Event

When an Orienteering club runs an event, the situation is quite different. While meetings and training sessions and occasional social activities may be pleasant experiences for the members of an Orienteering club, it is the excitement of regular Orienteering events that holds them together and keeps their interest alive. The more often these events take place and the more challenging they are, the more lively the club.

In a small club a few enthusiastic orienteers can arrange an Orienteering race in a few days' time. For a larger event in an ambitious club far more planning and preparation are necessary and many more people will be involved. Large international events and the Orienteering World Championships take years of planning and preparation. You can imagine the organization needed for the five-day Orienteering races held in Sweden in which up to 10,000 orienteers participate in 40 different classes.

But whatever the scope and size of the event, its ultimate success depends on a single person: the *course setter*. He determines the terrain, selects the control points, and lays out the course. If the course is good, the event will be good.

So it is first and foremost a matter of finding an experienced and imaginative course setter, then for others to back his efforts to the hilt in scheduling, promoting, and running the event. For larger events with many classes and participants, there has to be a team of course setters working together.

SETTING AN ORIENTEERING EVENT

If you are a member of an active Orienteering club and have proved yourself a skilled orienteer, sooner or later you may be called upon to act as a course setter for an event scheduled by your club. In accepting, you will be undertaking the most challenging involvement in Orienteering—also the most enjoyable part. Whereas, as an active orienteer, your task was to solve problems set by someone else for finding your way from control to control, it is now up to you to create problems for others to solve—problems in Orienteering that are interesting, challenging, and fair. So you recruit a couple of enthusiastic helpers and go to work. Other members of your club will assume the responsibility of establishing and manning start and finish areas, of acting as registrars, recorders, and other officials to permit you to concentrate on your task.

Selection of Territory

Your first task as course setter is to select an area for the event. To be considered suitable the territory should contain landscape features that will require the use of all the skills of good Orienteering in a degree of difficulty to fit the abilities of the participants. Beyond that, its use must be secured and maps of it must be available.

Suitable Territory

The territory for an Orienteering event should be of a well-wooded, undulating nature, preferably with little or no human habitation. It should be virgin ground as far as possible, particularly in the case of a large competition, so that certain participants are not favored by their familiarity with the area. A state or county park, possibly surrounded by large land holdings, might be considered ideal.

The territory should be well supplied with readily identifiable natural or man-made features suitable for control locations and attack points. But it should also be of such character that accidents are unlikely to occur—an area with dangerous slopes, quarry pits, bogs, and the like would be unsuitable.

The territory should have prominent well-defined boundaries, such as a main road, a railroad track, or a river; or it should contain roads by which anyone going astray or dropping out of the competition can locate the finish point without too much difficulty. Such "escape lines" are particularly important in the case of beginners or very young orienteers: they will know that by traveling a given "safety bearing," easily determined by compass, they will quickly get back to civilization. Exceptions to this rule may be made in competitions for Orienteering experts who may be expected to find their way under all circumstances.

Finally, the territory should provide a start area with space for parking and some arrangement for storing equipment and personal belongings. The finish area should have accommodations for washing up after the race, with showers if at all possible. Toilet facilities should be available at both the start and finish areas.

Permission of Land Owners

Before undertaking any extensive work in connection with setting the course, you, as course setter, should make certain that whoever owns the territory or has control over it will permit its use for Orienteering on the day scheduled. This applies also to public lands.

In some instances permission may be granted on the basis of a written request. In other cases, you may have to use a direct, personal appeal. In such cases, permission will generally be granted if the request is properly presented, the activity is thoroughly explained, and assurance is given of adherence to limitations set on use of the grounds.

Map of Territory

For competitive Orienteering, it is imperative that a good map of the territory be secured.

For the preliminary steps in course setting, a 1:24,000 Geological Survey map of the area should suffice. In the case of state or county parks, the departments concerned usually have maps available.

For the use of the participants on the day of the event, it may very well be that special maps must be prepared, based on maps available, with necessary corrections for subtractions and additions that have been made since the original map was produced. (See page 189 for Maps for Orienteering.) The regular topographic maps may be good enough in most areas, but map improvements with more details— whenever possible—make Orienteering more interesting and fun.

Setting the Course—Desk Work

With the territory picked, permissions granted, and map secured you are ready to get to work.

The actual course setting begins at your desk.

Start by studying the map of the territory. If you are an expert orienteer, the symbols on the map will seem to take three-dimensional shape. The contour lines will rise into hills and mountains. The wooded areas will take on color and form. The black lines will become paths and roads, railroad tracks and power lines. The blue markings will turn into winding rivers or quiet lakes.

Using your imagination, scan the map for the most significant and most challenging control points the territory has to offer. Set about marking such locations in as many different variations of the landscape as possible. If you are a smart course setter you won't mark the map directly. You will place the map in a clear plastic folder and do your marking on this with a red grease pencil that rubs off easily with a piece of tissue paper. Or you may use several plastic sheets that will make it possible for you to retain your markings as you change your mind from one grouping of controls to another, from one tentative course to another.

Due to the free nature of Orienteering there are no absolute rules that dictate the form and character of the course, except for events sanctioned by a national Orienteering association, championships, or international events. Otherwise, there are no absolute standards for the length of the course, for the distances between control points, or

or the number or placement of the controls. The creation of a course
s left to the course setter with due consideration of the participants'
bilities and ages. The quality of the course depends on the course
etter's Orienteering knowledge, his imagination, and his judgment,
lthough his decisions will also be governed by the suitability of the
errain.

Nevertheless, there are certain considerations that should always be
ept in mind.

General Considerations

Orienteering vs. Running—First of all, since the expert use of map and
ompass is the dominant test in an Orienteering event, the course
hould be set in such a way that it challenges the mental ability of
sing the skills of Orienteering rather than the physical ability of
ross-country running.

Variety—A good course will offer variety. It should afford opportu-
ities for both map reading and running by compass, but the empha-
is should be kept on using the map, with the compass a secondary
ool. It should provide possibilities for racing through all kinds of ter-
ain—through forests, along roads and paths, over fields and
meadows, and over or around hills, but with forest traveling the pre-
ominating feature. The legs between controls should be of different
engths, the controls of varying difficulty.

Route Choice—But more important than anything else, the course
or an Orienteering event should provide the participant with the
reatest possible challenge in selecting his own routes and finding his
wn way from one control to the next. The choice of route is the *alpha*
nd *omega* of Orienteering. It is here that the Orienteering enthusiast's
ngenuity and powers of concentrated thinking are subjected to the
everest test.

Difficulty of Course—Finally, the course must be adapted to the abil-
y and age of the participants. Expert orienteers will expect a

rugged course of a demanding length with many challenging control points, whereas juniors and beginners will need a course that is shor in length with only a few easy-to-find control points. Generally, th following table may suggest suitable course lengths and numbers o controls for different age groups, although special ability may mea that a competitor should enter a more difficult course than age alon indicates:

Class	Course	Miles	Kilometers	Numbers of Controls and Character
Beginners and Wayfarers	White	1–1½	1½–2½	3–5, easy to find
Girls 14–16 years Boys under 14	Yellow	2–3	3½–4½	4–7, easy and average
Girls 17–19 and over 35 Boys 15–16 and Men over 50	Orange	2–3	3½–4½	4–7, more difficul
Women over 20 Men 17–19 and 40–50	Red	4–5	6½–8	7–10, average and difficult
Men over 21	Blue	5–8	8–12	9–12, difficult

Control and Attack Points

The controls on a course should be located at objects that will giv the participants different kinds of tests. Some of the controls may k placed at certain elevation features, others at man-made features, sti others at water features—each of them requiring a special techniqu for reaching it.

The actual control points you choose will depend on the class o orienteers with whom you deal. For advanced orienteers suitabl control points may be: "Reentrant," "Depression," or "Knoll." Fc

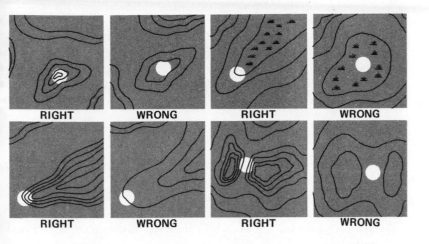

| RIGHT | WRONG | RIGHT | WRONG |
| RIGHT | WRONG | RIGHT | WRONG |

Pick suitable control points. Rights would be decided hilltop, tip of marsh or hill, decided col. Wrongs would be too flat features, middle of marsh.

beginners and juniors, more appropriate points would be: "Hilltop," "Bridge," or "Crossroad."

In a similar way, the expert may be able to get along with a fairly obscure attack point, whereas the less experienced orienteer will need one or more obvious landscape features for his attack.

The map segments on page 185, with their 5-mm circles, show the most commonly selected control points for Orienteering. For the sake of simplicity, they are separated into man-made, water, and elevation features. The descriptions of them as used by orienteers may need a bit of elucidation:

COL (SADDLE)—a saddle-shaped dip between two hills or in the crest of a ridge.

DEPRESSION—a low point in the ground, surrounded by higher ground, shown on the map by one or more closed contours with small "ticks"—hachures—pointing downward from the contours.

HILL—an elevation, shown by two or more closed contours.

KNOLL—a small hill, shown by a single closed contour.

Neck—a pinched-in section of a ridge.

Niche—a hollow in a hillside, shown by a contour kink.

Pass—a passable depression between two large hills or mountains.

Pond—a small body of water, less then 25 yards across.

Pulpit—a projection from a hillside, shown by a contour kink.

Ravine—a narrow, steep-side valley, shown by close parallel contours.

Reentrant—a minor side valley off a main valley, shown by one or more V-shaped contours.

Ridge—the elongated spine of a hill, shown by one or more long, closed contours with almost parallel sidelines.

Spur—a minor ridge jutting out from a main ridge and generally flanked by reentrants, shown by one or more U-shaped contours.

Summit—the actual top of a hill, indicated by at least two closed contours.

Track—term used in Orienteering for an unimproved dirt road, shown by parallel dashed lines.

Trail—equivalent to path, shown by a single dashed line.

Valley—an elongated area of low ground between two ridges, shown by wide-apart, more or less parallel contours.

(NOTE: In some countries, landscape features not found on the map are sometimes used as control points. In such cases, the description of a feature on the ground but not on the map is given with the indefinite article in front—A Bridge—while the description of a feature found on the ground and on the map is preceded by the definite article—THE Bridge. Such ambiguity should be avoided. All control points should be clearly indicated on the maps used by the orienteers, making the addition of an article in the description unnecessary: simply BRIDGE.)

There are, of course, several other landscape features shown on the map that may be used as control points, such as: Church, Cemetery, Quarry, Marsh, Dam, Cut, Fill, Trail Crossing, and others.

Before settling on the control points, consider carefully the function of a control: a control is the means to an end, it is not the end itself. In the same way that hitting the bull's-eye of a target demands expert marksmanship of a marksman, reaching a control point should de-

COMMONLY USED CONTROL POINTS

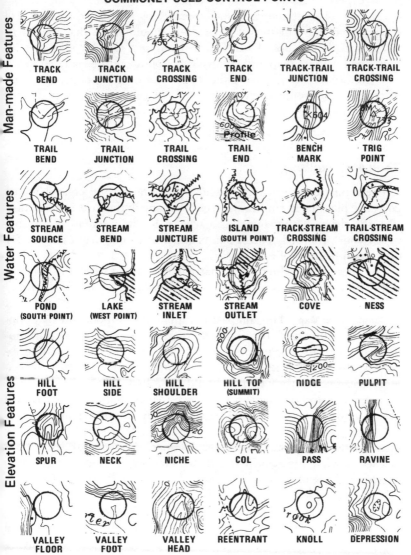

Man-made Features

TRACK BEND · TRACK JUNCTION · TRACK CROSSING · TRACK END · TRACK-TRAIL JUNCTION · TRACK-TRAIL CROSSING

TRAIL BEND · TRAIL JUNCTION · TRAIL CROSSING · TRAIL END · BENCH MARK · TRIG POINT

Water Features

STREAM SOURCE · STREAM BEND · STREAM JUNCTURE · ISLAND (SOUTH POINT) · TRACK-STREAM CROSSING · TRAIL-STREAM CROSSING

POND (SOUTH POINT) · LAKE (WEST POINT) · STREAM INLET · STREAM OUTLET · COVE · NESS

Elevation Features

HILL FOOT · HILL SIDE · HILL SHOULDER · HILL TOP (SUMMIT) · RIDGE · PULPIT

SPUR · NECK · NICHE · COL · PASS · RAVINE

VALLEY FLOOR · VALLEY FOOT · VALLEY HEAD · REENTRANT · KNOLL · DEPRESSION

Points used for controls may be man-made features, water features, or elevation features. Most of the above captions are self-explanatory. For description of the less common features, see explanations on pages 183–84.

mand expert Orienteering of an orienteer. It is what happens between controls that counts in an Orienteering race. Finding a control should never be a matter of chance—it should mean that the orienteer has made full use of his skill in reading a map for choosing his route, and using a map and compass for following the route chosen.

Therefore, before finalizing the location of control points, you need to consider the route choices that each of the controls provides for reaching the next.

Choice of Routes

The numerical sequence in which you line up the control points you have picked determines the legs from one to the next and, eventually, the shape of the course as a whole. So draw tentative lines between your proposed control points and study your map carefully for the terrain features of each leg.

The more route choices the participant has between the controls and the more demands on his map-reading skills, the better the leg.

Compass vs. Map—The compass is supposed to support the map, not take over its function. If the direct compass route from control number 4 to control 5, for instance, is not only the shortest route but obviously also the quickest, not necessitating any choice whatever, another location for the control should be found. It is only on a rare occasion and over a very short distance that a good course setter will permit a control to be reached by running by compass alone.

On the other hand, if direct compass leads over a steep hill or through dense forest, the direct compass becomes an important "choice of route" as against the choice of paths or contours that may lead around the obstacle.

Doglegs—Great care should be taken that the leg leading to a control does not make a sharp angle with the leg leading away from it toward the next control. Such a dogleg gives the late-comers a distinct advantage over the runners preceding them. The earlier runners will give away the location of the control as they continue toward the next.

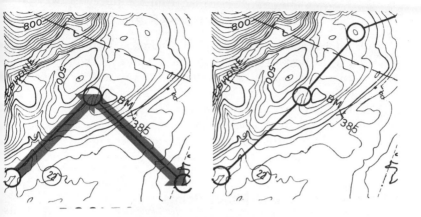

Don't pick control points that will create a dogleg and force early-arriving orienteers to give away the location to late-comers.

Handrails—While the use of handrails is permissible for the runner, a leg that follows a handrail too closely should be avoided.

Catching Features—A large catching feature—such as a road, a river, or a lake—invariably suggests "full speed ahead" by compass alone. To prevent such unthinking running by compass over a long distance, referred to in international Orienteering as "lost kilometers," the control should never be located on the far side of and close to the catching feature. It should be placed on the near side, as the runner approaches the feature, by a couple of hundred feet or more. This will require the orienteer to make full use of all his Orienteering skills instead of depending solely on his compass and running ability. If he decides to run full speed to the catching feature and then go back to the control, he penalizes himself through loss of time.

Hazards—No route choice that a runner may decide on because it looks the shortest or the quickest should ever involve any hazardous risks—such as a falling-rock area or a boggy lakeshore. If such a choice seems possible, another location should be picked for the next control.

Setting the Course—Field Work

With all considerations given full attention, your course setting shifts from the desk to the field for the purpose of finding out if the theoretical course you set at the desk can be turned into a practical course in the field.

The most important parts of field work are to determine that the tentatively chosen control points are suitable; that the attack points are usable; and that control and attack points are found in the field exactly where the map indicates they are located.

Checking Control and Attack Points

There is nothing that spoils a day for an orienteer so much as a course in which even one single control has been incorrectly placed, causing him to wander about without being able to locate it through no fault of his own. Orienteering is not a treasure hunt or a game of hide-and-seek but a sport that calls for fair play under all conditions.

Consequently, it is necessary for you, as course setter, not merely to sketch out a course on the map but to go over the ground yourself and reconnoiter it. It is your duty to ascertain that the locations you have chosen for controls are clearly identifiable features that are actually found where the map shows them to be. If the map does not agree with a proposed control location, the location should be abandoned and another chosen. It is also your duty to make certain that attack points from which an orienteer might be expected to reach the control are correctly indicated on the map. Much of this checking needs to be done by precision compass and pace counting.

As you check each of the control locations, tie a colored streamer to a nearby object. This will simplify matters when you come back to place the control markers just before the event.

Checking the Map

The ideal map for Orienteering is one that is an exact replica of the terrain in reduced scale. Or, to say it differently, the map should mirror the terrain. Such maps are rare! It is difficult to produce maps that are correct in every detail. From the time the map was made to the time you use it, several changes may have taken place in the landscaping: new roads may have been constructed and old ones abandoned; new houses may have been built, old ones torn down; certain woods may have become fields or vice versa; lakes may have turned into swamps or swamps into lakes.

Where such changes do not influence the choice of routes or the locations of controls you need make no changes in your dispositions. But where important changes have taken place—the tearing down of a bridge, for instance, and its rebuilding in a different location—updates obviously must be made on the master map and on the maps the participants will use.

Finalizing the Course

The necessary field work probably cannot be accomplished on a single reconnoitering expedition. You may need several. Each expedition will give you new ideas that may change your original concept. Make the necessary alterations, finalize the control locations, and number them in the order in which they are to be visited. Then write a description list telling the nature of each control, including a code number (in parentheses) which matches the code on the marker. Each participant can then check to make certain he is at the right control.

As a final check, go over the whole course alone or with one of your helpers. In the latter case, have your helper do the leading, acting as a course checker. (For a major event, an official course checker, or, as the British call him, a "course vetter," is required to do the final checking.)

Maps for Orienteering

The maps needed for an Orienteering event consist of a map of the area for each participant, and master maps from which the participants copy onto their own maps the course they have to follow and the controls they have to visit. The use of master maps can be eliminated by preprinting or marking the courses on the participants' maps.

Participants' Maps

Each participant should be provided with a map of the course area. The cost of the map may be included in the entry fee (see page 194, Invitation to Compete). The participant's map can be:

a regular government topographic map of the territory;
a similar topographic map published by the state or the county;
a reproduction of such maps, possibly somewhat improved, black-and-white or colored; or
a special Orienteering map.

If finances permit, you may want to provide each participant with a topographic map. A more feasible method will be to have black-and-white reproductions made from such maps of the section that covers the course area. To do this, certain preparations have to be made.

Since the blue color of lakes and streams on a topographic map do not photograph well or at all, begin by hatching the lakes with straight black lines and drawing wiggly lines over the water courses. Then have a photostat or PMT (photo mechanical transfer) print made of the area, preferably enlarging the original map from 1:24,000 or whatever scale it is to 1:12,000 (1 inch equal to 1,000 feet). Be sure to include on the photostat the scale rule from the margin of the map.

Paste up the photostat on a piece of cardboard. Add necessary marginal information: name of territory, name of event, scale in fraction, contour intervals, and any special instructions—such as "Not all paths shown. Not all buildings indicated." Draw in with black ink or blank out with white watercolor any corrections that seem necessary. Provide the map with magnetic north-south lines one inch apart.

Have a sufficient number of the completed map produced by offset or electronic reproduction (Xerox or other).

Special Orienteering Maps

It may take a great deal of experience before you or your club decide to take on the project of making special Orienteering maps. But you may eventually get there. Such maps make Orienteering still more exciting and fun. They further increase the importance of good navigation skills and fast decision-making by the participants. The Orienteering maps have been developed under the guidance of the International Orienteering Federation (I.O.F.). They are much more precise and detailed than regular topographic maps and are produced in larger scale (1:5,000 to 1:20,000).

Orienteering maps are based on base maps with precise contour lines drawn from aerial photographs by modern photogrammetric methods. The base map will also show some major features like lakes, creeks, roads, highways, and some trails and buildings. The completion of the map then requires substantial field work to find and locate on the map every terrain feature: small knolls, depressions, boulders, paths and trails, ditches, fence lines, etc.

Orienteering maps are used for championship events and international meets. You will find a sample of an Orienteering map in the envelope inside the back cover of the book. For up-to-date information on the availability of such maps in North America—which is limited but steadily increasing—contact the appropriate Orienteering Federation at the address given on page 210. There you can also get information about handbooks on how to make Orienteering maps.

Master Maps

For producing the necessary master maps, first turn your own map into a master map. To do this, use a red ball-point pen, a template with cutouts for circles (available in art shops), and a ruler.

Using template and pen, circle each control location with a red circle, 5 mm (0.5 cm) in diameter, in such a way that the exact—but unmarked—center of the circle is the exact location of the control. Draw a small triangle to show the location of the master maps—the actual start of the event. Draw two concentric circles, 5 mm and 7 mm, to indicate the finish. For a Cross-Country Orienteering event, number the control points in the order in which they are to be visited and connect them numerically with straight red lines. For Score Orienteering, mark the map with the score value of each control.

From this master's master map, copy as many master maps for the map area as are required by the number of participants. If there are, say, 100 participants in one class of a competition, you will need several copies of that class's master map. Otherwise the participants will delay one another while copying the maps.

Control Markers for Orienteering

One more job—an exceedingly important and demanding one—and your job as course setter is completed: on the morning of the event or, if feasible, on the day before, place the control markers in position.

Control Markers

The internationally recognized control marker for Orienteering events consists of three squares, 30 cm by 30 cm (12 inches by 12 inches), divided diagonally bottom left to top right into two triangles, the top left-hand triangle white, the bottom right-hand orange-red, joined together to form a hollow prism. Each control is identified by a code: a letter or number (never less than 30), black, 6 to 10 cm high (2½ to 4 inches), line width 6 to 10 mm (¼ to ⅜ inch). The control marker is suspended from cords in the upper corners. Such control markers, made from weatherproof cardboard and from lightweight nylon, are available through the Orienteering Services.

If you prefer, you can make your own control markers. A cardboard box, 12 inches high, 24 inches long, and 12 inches or more wide, will provide the materials for two markers. Three standard-size white vinyl floor tiles will make one marker—simply paint each tile with a red triangle and tie all three tiles into a prism with cord or wire them together with picture wire. Provide the markers with numbers.

For an informal Orienteering event or for reasons of economy, you can turn one-gallon bleach bottles or one-gallon milk cartons into control markers by painting them in the standard pattern.

Using a piece of strong cord, attach to each control marker a pin punch ("clipper") or a self-inking stamp with the code—number or letter—of the control. The participant uses this piece of equipment to punch or stamp his scorecard.

Placing the Control Markers

Each control marker must be put up in the exact location shown on

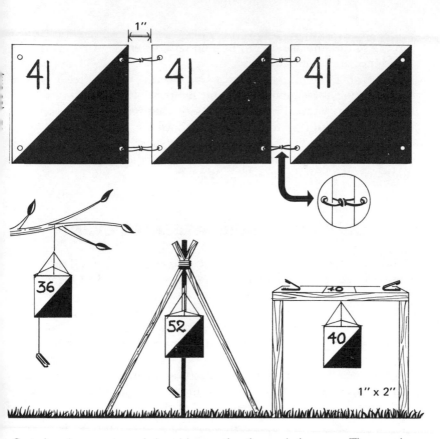

Control markers may be made by wiring together three 12-inch squares. They may be hung in trees, on tripods, or from a cross-piece between uprights.

the master map. It must be right there when the participant arrives and it must be clearly visible from all directions as he gets near to it.

Generally, the marker should be hanging approximately at waist height. If hung in a tree, it should be at a point of a branch far from the trunk so that the trunk does not hide it. If no natural support is found, it may be hung from a cord suspended between two trees, or from a tripod, or from a cross-piece between two uprights placed on the exact location. If the control is "Summit of Hill," eye-level height may proclaim its presence from too far a distance; a low position is proper so that the marker can be seen only when the participant is in its immediate vicinity.

A warning: the brightly colored Orienteering markers seem to have a devastating attraction for "souvenir hunters." If the territory is such that children or casual passers-by may see and remove the marker, the control point must, of necessity, be manned.

In any event, you, as course setter, must be positive that all markers are in position when, one hour before the start, you announce to the competition director "Go ahead!"

RUNNING AN ORIENTEERING EVENT

While the course setter has been busy setting the course and preparing master maps and description sheets, other officials of the Orienteering club, one of them acting as general *competition director*, have been taking care of their assigned duties. Some of these tasks are preliminary preparations: sending out invitations; acknowledging and numbering entries; mailing final information; and possibly securing prizes. The other arrangements take place the day of the event: setting up the registration desk at the assembly area; setting up and manning the "calling-up" area, the start location, the master-map area, and the finish; and possibly also manning some or all of the controls.

Preliminary Arrangements

Invitations to Compete

Before every important Orienteering event invitations to participate should be sent out to clubs and other organizations and, if desired, to interested individuals. This should be done early—certainly not later than a month before the proposed date. In the case of minor events—a club competition or other small-scale match—a brief notice in the form of an announcement at the regular club meeting, telephone communication, or a notice on the club bulletin board may be all that will be required.

Invitations or notices of an Orienteering event should contain the following information (see invitation, page 154):

1. Nature of the event (Cross-Country Orienteering, Score, Relay, etc.).
2. Date and hour of the event.
3. General area of the event and map information.
4. Class divisions and course lengths for the different classes.
5. Date the entries should be received by the organizers.
6. Entry fee, if any.
7. Name and address of organizing club or committee.

Signing Up Participants

As soon as entries start flowing in, the secretary of the organizing club writes out a control card for each entry, with name, club or team, start number, and class.

One week before the event the secretary may mail out additional final instructions to each entry, informing the participant of the exact assembly point, his starting time, and whatever relevant information may be necessary regarding parking, clothing, changing, equipment, and special conditions (see page 154).

Day of Orienteering Event

Assembly Area

As soon as a participant has arrived in the assembly area, has parked his car, and has changed into his running outfit, he signs in to the *registrar* at the registration desk. His name is checked off on the recorder's sheet and he is given his control card, which he will need throughout the race and which gives his starting time. He then has a chance to meet and talk to other participants about the race and to study the contents of the bulletin board which the organizing club may have put up. On this bulletin board he may find information on first aid arrangements, telephone numbers for emergencies, the time the day's events will finish, the time control markers will be removed,

RECORDING SHEET								
EVENT _____ PLACE _____ DATE _____								
NAME	No.	Team	Class	Start Time	Finish Time	Time Used	Controls Missed	Position

The recording sheet may be developed as shown above. The recorder records on it all the pertinent information relating to each participant.

and the safety bearing. The bulletin board may also contain a complete listing of the participants in the day's races and their starting times.

Start Area

Getting off on an Orienteering race is a double feature:

Calling up—Customarily, a participant is called to the start area by the official *caller* approximately five minutes before his starting time. The *control-card-stub collector* does what his name implies and the *map-pick-up checker* checks that he receives his map and description list of the control points and directs him to the actual starting line, unless premarked maps are used.

The Start—The ordinary way of starting consists of the participant moving up to the starting line where he is sent off by a blast from the *starter*'s whistle, as the *time keeper* calls out his departure time from a

The start area requires only a few officials to send off the orienteers. The most important feature is the recording of starting times.

stop watch and the *time recorder* writes it down on the recorder's sheet.

A better method gaining wide acceptance is to start the participants off on a three-minute basis (compare with description on page 156):

3 minutes before start: participant is called and enters the back row (the "Get in!" row) of the starting grid.

2 minutes before start: at a blast of the starter's whistle, the participant advances to the next row (the "Get ready!" row). Here he receives a copy of the description list, which describes the nature of the control points, and the map, unless premarked maps are used.

1 minute before start: at another whistle blast, the participant moves into the front row (the "Get set!" row). When maps premarked with the locations of the controls are used, they would be distributed here. (Note that the description list is necessary even if the maps are premarked. The participant should know the location and the nature of the controls.)

Zero minute: at a third blast from the whistle of the starter (for "Go!"), the participant takes off. The time keeper or time recorder records his departure time or checks it off against a prepared starting list.

Master-Map Area

Unless premarked maps are used, the first part of the course consists of a short trail—100 to 300 feet—marked with white, yellow, and red streamers (blue for an elite course) leading the participants to the correct maps for their courses in the master-map area. This trail is laid out so that the master-map area is out of sight of the start area.

Each participant follows the trail at full speed to the master map that has on it the course for his particular class. The master maps, as developed by the course setter, are mounted on pieces of plywood or other hard-wood and are protected against finger marks and possible precipitation by a sheet of plastic. The participant *very carefully* copies the control points and the course outline from the master map onto his own map.

As soon as that is done, the participant takes off from the master-map area, marked on the map with a small triangle, toward the first control, marked on the map with a small circle.

On the Course

The moment the participant leaves the master-map area, he is completely on his own. He follows the course using his utmost Orienteer-

FINISH

The finish area will require half a dozen or more officials. The number will depend on the number of orienteers taking part in the event.

ing skills for finding the controls in the order prescribed, and his running ability for getting through the course in the shortest possible time. At each control point he stamps or punches his control card in the proper square with the code symbol as proof of having visited it.

Finish Area

The finish area is usually located near the start area. There is no problem finding it: a trail marked by colored streamers leads directly to it from the final control point. The last few hundred feet of this trail runs through open terrain so the participant may put on a final spurt and arrive in style. This also permits the time keeper to see the participants as they approach the finish line and allows the spectators to watch the finish.

Score Taking—The moment a participant crosses the finish line—indicated by a banner inscribed with the word FINISH—the *time caller* calls out his time to the nearest second from a stop watch synchronized with the watch of the starting official. The *time recorder* writes down the time on his list as the participant turns his control card over to the *control-card collector* who carefully keeps the cards in proper

CLASS: Men's #1. COURSE: White. TIME: in hours, minutes, seconds. NO.: Starting number.

TOP PART of CONTROL CARD turned over to control-card-stub collector at START.

BOTTOM PART of CONTROL CARD carried by orienteer and punched at controls. Turned over to control-card collector at FINISH.

FINISH according to finish-line time recorder's watch. START according to start-line time recorder's watch. TIME used in minutes and seconds. Transferred to top.

PUNCH MARKS made at the control points.

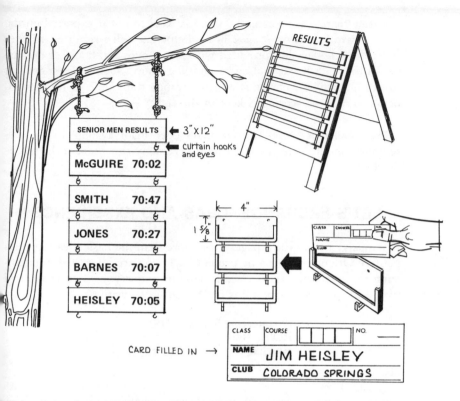

RESULTS

SENIOR MEN RESULTS ← 3"×12"

← curtain hooks and eyes

McGUIRE 70:02

SMITH 70:47

JONES 70:27

BARNES 70:07

HEISLEY 70:05

← 4" →

1 5⁄8"

CARD FILLED IN →

CLASS	COURSE			NO.
NAME	JIM HEISLEY			
CLUB	COLORADO SPRINGS			

The result board may consist of wooden slats hung up together or placed on a sheet of plywood, or of plastic frames hooked together.

order, according to the arrivals. The cards are picked up by the *results runner* who brings them, 10 or 15 at a time, depending on how close the participants come in, to the competition secretariat table. There the *recorder* puts the time onto his record sheet and makes a note whether the clipper marks for the controls are correct and in the right order. (If any controls are missed in a Cross-Country Orienteering race, the participant usually is disqualified, but an alternative is to penalize him by adding, for example, 30 minutes to his finishing time for each control missed.) The *scorer* (time calculator) works out the score based on minutes and seconds elapsed.

Result Board—As soon as the score is worked out it is posted on the result board by the *result judge* or his helpers. Such a result board may consist of wooden slats provided with screw eyes and hooks or of plastic frames with hooks and corresponding holes. Such an arrangement makes it possible to arrange and re-arrange the names of the participants so that the scoring is kept in the right order.

Presentation of Prizes—If prizes have been made available, their presentation should take place at a short ceremony the moment the race is finished.

LET'S EXCHANGE IDEAS AND EXPERIENCES

Obviously, within these pages little more than the basic ideas on competitive Orienteering can be presented. If you are interested in organizing Orienteering events for a local club or for your own group and would like further suggestions on this subject, write to:

> Orienteering Services/USA
> P.O.B. 1604
> Binghamton, New York 13902

or to:

> Orienteering Services/Canada
> 446 McNicoll Avenue
> Willowdale, Ontario, Canada M2H 2E1

and ask for a complete list of informative material, teaching aids, films, and so on. For your convenience, a business reply card is included in the envelope in the back of this book.

If you do run an Orienteering event, be sure to send a few words of comments on your experience to the Orienteering Service from which you received the suggestions.

The exchange of ideas and experiences is of the greatest importance in the promotion of

The Sport of ORIENTEERING.

ANSWERS TO TESTS

Map Symbol Quiz (page 28)

1. Road (improved dirt)
2. Contour lines (hill)
3. Cemeteries
4. Railroad (single track)
5. Spring
6. Well
7. Buildings
8. Bench mark (monumented)
9. Marsh
10. Trail
11. Bridge (river, road)
12. Triangulation station
13. River (streams)
14. Road (unimproved dirt)
15. Sand dunes
16. Church
17. School

Contour Quiz (pages 31–32)

1. (a) almost level
2. (a) from bottom of map to top of map
3. (b) a slow grade
4. (a) a slow-moving stream
5. (a) Hutton Hill
   (c) Niger Marsh
   (e) Huckleberry Mountain

Contour Matching (page 32)

A—6   B—1   C—4   D—3   E—2   F—5

Take Point Bearings (pages 39–40)

1. 73°   2. 297°   3. 50°   4. 274°   5. 160°
6. 168°   7. 126°   8. 183°   9. 160°   10. 346°

(Bearings are figured from the center of one landmark to the center of the other. Permissible error: two degrees more or less)

Direction Quiz (pages 43–44)

1. 358°   2. 97°   3. 252°   4. 80°   5. 106°

Distance Quiz (page 47)

1. 7,100 feet   2. 2,900 feet   3. 21,400 feet
4. 4,000   5. 12,200

(Distances are figured from the center of one landmark to the center of the other. Permissible error: 100 feet more or less)

FIND PLACES ON THE MAP (page 49)

1. Glenburnie
2. Crossroads (x 455)
3. Crossroads (432)
4. Church (cemetery)
5. Crossroads (432)
6. Hill 384
7. Road-T (441)
8. Road-Bend
9. Crossroads (455)
10. Start of stream

SCHOOLYARD COMPASS GAME (pages 83–85)

1. AEOUZP   2. EIULPA   3. IOLZAE   4. OUZPEI
5. ULPAIO   6. LZAEOU   7. ZPEIUL   8. PAIOLZ
9. AIUZAE   10. EOLPEI

COMPASS COMPETITION (pages 88–90)

Start Point 1:
  Destination Point 7
Start Point 3:
  Destination Point 2
Start Point 5:
  Destination Point 16
Start Point 7:
  Destination Point 8
Start Point 9:
  Destination Point 15

Start Point 2:
  Destination Point 19
Start Point 4:
  Destination Point 8
Start Point 6:
  Destination Point 8
Start Point 8:
  Destination Point 9
Start Point 10:
  Destination Point 19

COMPASS SETTING QUIZ (pages 107–8)

1. 94°   2. 4°   3. 292°   4. 262°   5. 224°

(Bearings are figured from the center of one landmark to the center of the other. Permissible error: two degrees more or less)

WHAT DO YOU FIND? (pages 108–9)

1. Church
2. Road-T, Glenburnie
3. Top of Record Hill
4. Road-T (381)
5. Marsh

GLOSSARY

AIMING OFF—a method by which the orienteer aims to one side of a control instead of directly at it (page 170).

ATTACK POINT—an easy-to-find feature shown on the map from which the final approach—"attack"—to the control may be made (page 163).

BACK-READING—looking back over the compass toward the point from which you came (page 78).

BASE PLATE—the rectangular plate of the Orienteering compass on which the compass housing is mounted (page 72).

BEARING—originally the nautical term for the direction of an object from the ship. In Orienteering defined as "a direction stated in compass degrees" (page 74).

CARDINAL POINTS—the four principal points of the compass: north, east, south, and west (page 72).

CATCHING FEATURE—a longish feature shown on the map running crosswise to the direction to be followed (page 164).

CHECKPOINT—a conspicuous feature in the landscape shown on the map, used by the orienteer to check his progress (page 165).

CLUECARD—see CONTROL DESCRIPTION.

COMPASS—instrument for determining directions with the help of a strip of magnetized steel swinging on a pivot (page 63).

COMPASS, CONVENTIONAL—a compass generally enclosed in a watchcase-type of housing (page 69).

COMPASS, ORIENTEERING—see ORIENTEERING COMPASS.

CONTOUR INTERVAL—the distance in height between one contour line and the one next to it (page 23).

CONTOUR LINE—an imaginary line in the field along which every point is at the same height above sea level (page 23).

CONTOURING—a method of traveling around an obstacle, such as a hill, by keeping at the same elevation, thus following a contour (page 166).

CONTROL—one of several locations in the field to be visited by the orienteer during an Orienteering event. Marked on the master map by a red circle, in the field by a prism-shaped red-and-white marker (page 182).

CONTROL CARD—a card carried by the orienteer, to be marked at designated controls in a prescribed sequence (pages 155 and 200).

CONTROL DESCRIPTION—a sheet or card with a brief explanation of the nature of the controls to be visited, with code numbers coinciding with the numbers on the control markers (pages 156 and 183).

CONTROL PUNCH—usually a pin punch, placed at a control, to be used in punching the control card as proof that the orienteer has visited the location (page 192).

CULTURAL FEATURES—man-made landscape features: roads, buildings, etc. (page 19).

DECLINATION—the angle between the direction the compass needle points and the true-north line; the difference in degrees between magnetic-north direction and true-north direction in any given locality (page 111).

DESCRIPTION SHEET—see CONTROL DESCRIPTION.

DIAL, COMPASS—the rim or edge of the compass housing, usually marked with the initials of the cardinal points and graduated in the 360 degrees of a circle (page 73).

DIRECTION—the relative location of one landscape feature to another (page 32). See also BEARING.

DIRECTION-OF-TRAVEL ARROW—the arrow on the base plate of the Orienteering compass which points in the direction of travel when the compass is oriented (pages 72–73).

HANDRAILS—a longish feature shown on the map running more or less parallel to the direction to be followed (page 163).

HOUSING—the part of the compass that "houses" the needle; on Orienteering compasses liquid-filled and turnable (page 72).

HYDROGRAPHIC FEATURES—water features: streams, lakes, etc. From Greek *hydro*, water and *graphein*, to write (pages 19, 22, and 136).

HYPSOGRAPHIC FEATURES—elevations: hills and valleys. From Greek *hypso*, height, and *graphein*, to write (pages 19 and 25).

INDEX POINTER—a line on the raised part of the base plate of the Orienteering compass against which the degree number of the dial on the compass housing is read (page 73).

INTERCARDINAL POINTS—the four points of the compass between the four CARDINAL POINTS: north-east, south-east, south-west, north-west.

I.O.F.—International Orienteering Federation.

LANDMARK—a feature in the landscape which can be readily recognized—anything from a prominent tree or rock, to a church or a lake.

LATITUDE—distance in degrees north and south from Equator (page 17).

LEG—a stretch of country to be negotiated between controls (page 158).

LONGITUDE—distance in degrees east and west from Greenwich, England (page 17).

MAGNETIC LINES—lines on an Orienteering map pointing to magnetic north (page 114).

MAGNETIC-NORTH—the direction to which the compass needle points (pages 110–11).

MAP—a reduced representation of a portion of the surface of the earth (page 8).

MAP SYMBOLS—small designs used on a map to indicate the features of a landscape (page 19).

MASTER MAP—a map on which the controls of an Orienteering event are marked and from which each orienteer marks his or her own map at the start (pages 157 and 191).

MERIDIANS—lines on the map or imaginary lines in the field running true north to true south (page 17).

ORIENTATION—the process of determining one's location in the field with the help of landscape features, map, or compass, or with all three combined.

ORIENTEER OR ORIENTEERER—a person who orienteers, that is, who participates in the sport of Orienteering. Both terms are used in the English language. "Orienteerer" is probably more correct linguistically and is the noun formed from the verb by adding the standard English agent termination of -er.

ORIENTEERING—the skill or the process of finding your way in the field with map and compass combined. A coined word and trademark registered by Orienteering Services to identify an outdoor program based on the use of map and compass, as well as to identify certain services rendered and products distributed by Orienteering Services for this sport.

ORIENTEERING COMPASS—a compass especially designed to simplify the process of finding your way with map and compass. Usually has its compass housing mounted on a rectangular base plate in such a way that it can be turned easily (page 72).

ORIENTING ARROW—arrow-marking or parallel lines in or on housing of Orienteering compass; used for setting the compass (page 72).

ORIENTING, COMPASS—holding compass in such a way that the directions of its dial coincide with the same directions in the field (pages 74 and 78).

ORIENTING LINES OF COMPASS—the lines on the inside bottom of the compass housing parallel to the N-S orienting arrow of the compass housing; also called "magnetic-north lines" or "compass meridian lines."

ORIENTING, MAP—turning map in such a way that what is north on the map corresponds with north in the field. Done by "inspection" (page 52), or with the help of a compass (pages 118–19).

PACE—double-step (page 53).

PACE COUNTING—measuring distance by counting the number of double-steps taken (page 173).

PACE SCALE—a special scale giving the number of paces to take for a measured distance on the map, selected for the individual and based on his step length (page 174).

PROTRACTOR—instrument used for measuring angles, usually in degrees (page 37).

QUADRANGLE—a rectangular tract of land depicted on a map (page 12).

ROUTE—the way taken between two control points (page 162).

SCALE—the proportion between a distance on the map and the actual distance in the field (page 9).

SILVA®—trademark registered by Silva Co. Used to identify Orienteering compasses and other types of high grade compasses.

STEERING MARK—an easily identifiable feature in the landscape not shown on the map, used by the orienteer to follow a bearing (page 169).

TOPOGRAPHIC MAPS—maps of high precision. From the Greek *topos*, place, and *graphein*, to write (page 9).

VARIATION—another term for DECLINATION.

WAYFARING—a leisurely form of Orienteering in which enjoyment of nature takes precedence over the competitive aspects of the sport (page 148).

VALUABLE ADDRESSES

For information on Teaching and Training Aids (like practicing compasses and protractors, training maps, compass training demonstrators, etc.) and on other textbooks, write to:

Orienteering Services/U.S.A.
P.O.B. 1604
Binghamton, New York 13902

In Canada:

Orienteering Services/ Canada
446 McNicoll Avenue
Willowdale, Ontario, Canada M2H 2E1

For information about films on map-and-compass use and on Orienteering, write to:

The International Film Bureau
332 South Michigan Avenue
Chicago, Illinois 60604

In Canada:

Educational Film Distributors Ltd.
285 Lesmill Road
Don Mills, Ontario, Canada M3B 2V1

For information on Competitive Orienteering Racing in the U.S.A. write to:

U. S. Orienteering Federation
P. O. B. 1039
Ballwin, MO 63011

In Canada:

The Canadian Orienteering Federation
P.O.B. #6206
Terminal A, Toronto 1, Canada

INDEX

Aiming off, 170
Air compass. *See* Standard compass

Backpacking skills, 132
Back-reading, 93
Bar scale, 44
Base plate, 72–73
Beeline out-and-back compass walk,
  92–93

Canoeing skills, 133–34
Catching features, 164
Checkpoints, 165
Clothes for Orienteering, 122
Compass, 2–5
  beeline walk, 92–93
  conventional. *See* Conventional
    compass
  declination, 109–14
  development of, 64–66
  for fishermen, 97–102
  history of, 63–64
  for hunters, 100–102
  needle, 64
  Orienteering. *See* Orienteering
    compass
  overcoming obstacles, 93–97
  parts of, 72–73
  practice. *See* Practice and games
  setting, 105–6
  three-legged compass walk, 80–82
  traveling by, 69–71, 80–102
  types of, 64–66
Compass housing, 72
Competitive Orienteering, 139–202
  field, assists in, 163–65
  following routes, 168–76
  overcoming obstacles, 165–67
  route, finalizing, 167–68
  routes, choice of, 162–67
  types of, 141–53

Contour interval, 23–24
Contour lines, 22–26
Control markers, 192–94
Conventional compass
  finding directions with, 69–70
  following directions with, 70–71
  original location, returning to, 71
  use of, 69–71

Declination
  importance of, 111–12
  resetting compass for, 113–14
Directions, map, 32–42
  finding, with an Orienteering com-
    pass, 40–42
  finding, with a paper circle protrac-
    tor, 35–37
  finding with a protractor, 37–40
Distances, map
  determining, 52–54
  map measures, 46–47
  map's bar scale, use of, 44
Double-steps, 53

Equipment for Orienteering, 122

Fishing
  finding fishing lake, 97–98
  relocating fishing spot, 98–100

Handrails, 163–64
Hiking skills, 132
Hunting
  general direction, 100–101
  pinpointing kill, 101–2

Index contour line, 23
Induction-dampened compasses, 64
Intermediate contour lines, 23

Latitude, 10–11
Liquid-filled compasses, 66
Longitude, 10–11

Magnetic needle, 72
Map measures, 46–47
Maps, 2–5
  bar scales, 44
  Canadian, 13
  compass language and, 114–17
  dates on, 18–19, 54–55
  defined, 8
  description, 15–19
  designations, 47–49
  details, 19–32
  directions, 32–42
  games. *See* Practices and games
  kinds, 8–9
  location, 16–18
  name of map area, 15–16
  orienting, 51–52
  practice. *See* Practice and games
  scale, 9–11
  state, 8–9
  symbols, 8
  topographic, 9
  traveling, 50–57
  United States maps, 12–13
  walk, 50–51, 57–58
  what maps tell, 14–19
Map symbols
  elevation features, 22–26
  man-made features, 19–32
  vegetation features, 22
  water features, 22–23, 136
Master maps, 157, 191–92
Meridian lines, 10

Orienteering
  art of, 1–6
  compass declination, 109–14
  control markers for, 192–94
  distances and, 106–7

getting ready for, 117–19
hike, 122–31
maps for, 189–92
Point-to-Point. *See* Point-to-Point
  Orienteering
precision. *See* Precision Orienteering
Preset-Course. *See* Preset-Course
  Orienteering
romance of, 5–6
Rough. *See* Rough Orienteering
as a sport, 140–41
steps in, 124–27
territory, selection of, 178–80
trip, at home, 104–9
using map and compass in, 119–22
Wilderness. *See* Wilderness Orienteering
Orienteering compass, 66
  finding bearings with, 73–74
  finding directions with, 40–42
  following bearing with, 77–78
  original location, returning to,
    78–79
  parts of, 72–73
  as protractor, 42–43
  as ruler, 45–46
  use of, 71–74
Orienteering event
  assembly area, 195–96
  finish area, 199–202
  master-map area, 198
  on the course, 198
  organizing, 176–78
  routes, choice of, 186–87
  running, 194–95
  setting, 178–94
  setting the course—desk work,
    180–87
  setting the course—field work,
    188–89
  start area, 196–98
Orienteering race, 153–62

"*Orienteering*" ®
COMPASSES

Ask your dealer to demonstrate the different SILVA® models or write for complete information by using the convenient post card in the envelope on the inside back cover of this book.

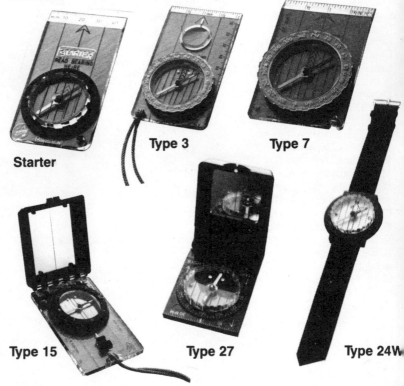

Starter

Type 3

Type 7

Type 15

Type 27

Type 24W

Orienteering® films available: BY MAP AND COMPASS, ORIENTEERING® and THE INVISIBLE FORCE OF DIRECTION, WHAT MAKES THEM RUN and other films. For information write to the film distributors for U.S.A. and Canada at the addresses on page 210.